A SKATING LIFE

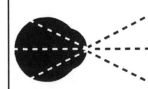

This Large Print Book carries the
Seal of Approval of N.A.V.H.

A SKATING LIFE

DOROTHY HAMILL
WITH DEBORAH AMELON

THORNDIKE PRESS

An imprint of Thomson Gale, a part of The Thomson Corporation

Detroit • New York • San Francisco • New Haven, Conn. • Waterville, Maine • London

Thorndike Press, an imprint of The Gale Group.

Thomson and Star Logo and Thorndike are trademarks and Gale is a registered trademark used herein under license.

Thorndike Press® Large Print Biography.

The text of this Large Print edition is unabridged.

Other aspects of the book may vary from the original edition.

Set in 16 pt. Plantin.

LIBRARY OF CONGRESS CATALOGING-IN-PUBLICATION DATA

Hamill, Dorothy.
    A skating life / by Dorothy Hamill as told to Deborah Amelon. — Large print ed.
      p. cm.
      ISBN-13: 978-0-7862-9965-2 (hbk. : alk. paper)
      ISBN-10: 0-7862-9965-7 (hbk. : alk. paper)
      1. Figure skaters — United States — Biography. 2. Women figure skaters — United States — Biography. 3. Large type books. [1. Hamill, Dorothy.]
I. Amelon, Deborah. II. Title.
GV850.H3A3 2007
796.91'2092—dc22
[B]

                            2007027909

Published in 2007 in arrangement with Hyperion,
an imprint of Buena Vista Books, Inc.

Printed in the United States of America on permanent paper
10 9 8 7 6 5 4 3 2 1

This book is for my daughter
and my parents.
I love you.

CONTENTS

PROLOGUE: Innsbruck, Austria . . . 9

1. How to Breed an Olympic
   Champion . . . Maybe? 15
2. The Lake Placid Years 28
3. Bright Lights, Big City Girl 65
4. Go West, Young Skater 108
5. This Way to the Olympics 152
6. Hollywood, Here I Come 174
7. The High Price of Gold 205
8. Love on the Run 228
9. Good-bye, Dean 264
10. Family Life . . . Finally 286
11. Escapades 302
12. Divorce, Dorothy Style 316
13. The Racehorse Back at the
    Starting Gate 332
14. Golden Snowflakes 349

ACKNOWLEDGMENTS 367

PROLOGUE:
INNSBRUCK, AUSTRIA

The hotel room was so thick with cigarette smoke we could barely make out my mother sitting in the middle of it. It was February 13, 1976, and I had just won the Olympic gold medal for ladies' figure skating. The group of us, my dad, sister, brother, and sister-in-law, had dashed back excitedly to tell my mother the results. She got up off her chair as if she'd not moved for hours and came closer to me.

"How did you do?" she asked.

"I won."

"That's nice, Dorothy."

She had not come to the arena to see me skate nor to watch the medal ceremony and, thirty years later, this still remains a mystery to me. I had run off the ice after I had skated and into my father's arms. We'd watched my scores being posted together as the joyous crowd threw bouquets of flowers on the ice. I went through the entire medal ceremony with mixed emotions. With my heart beating loudly, I was overwhelmingly proud hearing our national anthem and knowing that my decade of hard work had culminated in this most time-honored of victories. I felt it had all paid off for the numerous people who had helped me get here, to the highest step on the podium. I thought of my coaches, my father, my brother, sister, and all the many friends and relatives who had contributed in any way they could. Most of all, I thought of my mom. As thousands cheered in the arena, and millions more watched on TV, I was ecstatic sharing this experience with everyone who felt my joy. But I was also standing up there quite alone. I wondered where my mother was in the arena. I could not see her. And it wasn't because I wasn't wearing my glasses. I'd find out after the ceremony that she wasn't there.

My mother is the most giving, self-sacrificing woman I have ever known, but I've always been confused by her. One would think an Olympic gold medal around my neck would erase the pain our relationship caused me, but I seemed to feel it more intensely than ever. Here was the woman most closely responsible for my success, who had watched me at almost every practice, overseen every decision, and had not only changed her life for me but altered her entire being to help me become the best skater I could. Her years of unflinching devotion to my goal were finally fulfilled, yet she could not express happiness for me. Nor for herself.

The emotion I felt walking into that Innsbruck hotel room and hearing my mom's impassive response, "That's nice," for winning an Olympic gold medal actually began years before our arrival in Innsbruck. I wondered at that time how we could have come to this, a mother and daughter with lives so intertwined but so estranged. I couldn't possibly have known then that the battleground of our relationship was just the beginning of a series of obstacles that would begin after my winning the Olympics. It has taken me years to realize that this battleground had its roots planted long before I was born. I could have chosen to let it stop me from achieving my goals or I could use it to spur me on. It has always been my choice, even though I didn't know it at the time. The lessons I learned along the way, and continue to learn, go far beyond the edge of an ice rink.

A SKATING LIFE

1
HOW TO BREED AN OLYMPIC CHAMPION . . . MAYBE?

Our family life, before figure skating turned it upside down, seemed normal. Our town of Riverside, Connecticut, was part of Greenwich and we had the advantage of their wonderful community, with great beaches and beautiful parks. Many of my relatives and friends of my parents kept boats on the Long Island Sound; my dad loved the water and he wanted us to have one too. We bought the best one we could afford, a third-hand cabin cruiser. As a family, we decided to name it *On the Rocks,* a name that could have foretold my future because my parents had to sell it when I started the expensive sport of figure skating. We would all dock our boats together, and my cousins and I would run from boat to boat. So much of our lives revolved around the water. My family had a membership to the Riverside Yacht Club, where my brother, Sandy, learned to sail and I competed in local swim races. My sister,

Marcia, became a competitive springboard diver and my brother excelled in water polo. We would spend weekends at my maternal grandparents' summer home in Rockport, Massachusetts, just a couple miles from the ocean. Jonsie and Bill loved being with their grandchildren: They took us to historic landmarks and picnics at the beach, and treated us to lobster dinners (lobster was inexpensive in those days). Marcia, Sandy, and I would pick wild blueberries; my grandmother loved to bake them in muffins and pancakes, indulging our sweet tooth. We were so lucky, and had such fun running around and teasing one another. Between the Yacht Club, the boating life, and summering in Rockport, I was living a privileged childhood.

We were the all-American happy family. We'd play capture the flag and tag in our grassy front yard. Mom had her bridge parties at the house and there always seemed to be laughter. My brother concocted science experiments and kept us on edge with his results. Marcia practiced her ballet and I loved to copy her. I wanted to be just like her and always tried to tag along after her, so happy whenever she and her friends would let me play with them. Mom was not a good cook — she'd boil vegetables until they were gray

— so we looked forward to Swanson TV Dinners. But, with her great sense of humor, she took it in stride and laughed at herself. We had warm family gatherings, both at our house and my Aunt Zipper's large home in Stamford. I fondly remember singing around their fireplace, dining room table, or wherever, on every holiday.

Then there was the daily ritual when Dad would come home from work and indulge in cocktail hour, his generation's euphemism for suburban drinking. My father, Chalmers ("Chal"), was born into a family well known for their artistic and intellectual pursuits. He was the middle child of seven, the eldest son, whose father was a Princeton grad who went to Harvard Law School. Before his father started working for the Department of Justice in Washington, DC, he and his wife, Edna, raised their brood in White Plains, New York, at a time when there was no television. Families found other interests. Lucky for me, the Hamills found music. Growing up, Dad and his sisters loved to sing, especially as my father became more proficient on the piano and the clarinet. He never had a music lesson in his life, yet he taught himself to read and arrange music. At fifteen, my dad had his own band, but as the firstborn son, he was expected to enter into a traditional masculine career. He went to Princeton to become a civil engineer and also managed to develop his musical gifts. He wrote arrangements for the Princeton Nassoons, an a cappella singing group that exists at Princeton to this day. He so loved his work with the Nassoons that he continued to arrange music for them after his graduation (and the group so loved his work that they still perform his arrangements, fifty years later). Despite his obvious musical talent, he ran the government division at Pitney Bowes for thirty years to support his family.

Mom and Dad had their nightly cocktails together, to catch up on the events of the day. It wasn't any different from the drinking their parents had done to deal with the unspoken depression in both of their families. My mother, Carolyn (Carol), was raised in Newton, Massachusetts, with her one brother. She'd inherited a sense of adventure from her mother, Esther Jones, who had bravely ventured to the East Coast from her home in California to go to dental school, where she became a hygienist and met my grandfather, Willis Clough, a 1918 Harvard graduate. My mother was sent to an all-girl private high school in her junior year and it changed her life, giving her a sense of empowerment and independence at a crucial young age. Dana Hall in Wellesley, Massachusetts, expected all its girls to choose their own sports. They played on varsity teams in a league against other all-girl schools, thirty years before Title IX, when school sports were generally only for boys. Mom excelled at field hockey and basketball, not traditionally women's sports. My maternal grandmother played some golf but otherwise never had any opportunity to pursue sports. She must have seen something in her daughter and wished more for her — just as my mom wished more for me.

After Dana Hall, Mom went to the University of New Hampshire, where she had a rude awakening to the reality of women's sports: There weren't any. She didn't know what she was supposed to do with a college education, so she felt little sense of direction. Fortunately, there was one constant love in her life and she was able to pursue it in the summers. My mom loved horses and began teaching horseback riding and horse grooming at the Millbrook Camp in Maine. It was there that she met my father, in the summer of 1947, because Dad needed a job after coming back from the war. Neither of them could have guessed they each came from a family fraught with undiagnosed and untreated depression. To the outside world, their families were successful and happy. To each of them, it was something they wanted to believe.

My mom instantly admired my dad. She thought he was a fine, smart man. She fell in love with him that first summer. She loved his even disposition, how well he got along with everybody, how he was never critical nor demeaning. She loved his musicality, a trait she did not possess. She fell in love with his family, too. Coming from a small family, she felt enveloped in the happiness of his numerous family members. She discovered happiness she had never known, sitting in their home, enjoying their singing.

They were opposites attracting. Dad fell in love with her sense of humor. She could make him laugh and she was different from the other girls. She had a unique take on life and spoke her mind. She was strong, physically and mentally, and let no one boss her around. He loved how athletic she was and how she always insisted on outdoor physical activity. She regularly took him hiking into the mountains, a treat for a man whose vocations kept him indoors. They knew they were meant to be together and married in 1949. Mom was only twenty-three and Dad was a bright-eyed, eager twenty-seven. They dreamed of having a family, but they wanted to be responsible. They wanted to wait until Dad graduated and got a job.

A man musically gifted. A woman athletically inclined. Breeding ground for an Olympic figure skater? It never crossed their minds. Just as it never crossed their minds how their untreated depression would affect the family they wanted to create.

Life was never easy for them. After Dad's graduation they ended up in hot, dusty Gary, Indiana, so he could be in a training program for Inland Steel. He learned everything there was to know about open-hearth furnaces and came home every day covered in soot. Mom hated it. She couldn't stand the thought of her newborn son (Sandy, my brother) breathing in the sooty air, so she rallied, with the maternal instinct of a lioness protecting her cub, to get the young family out of Gary. Dad received an offer from Quaker Oats in Chicago, and my sister, Marcia, was born there. I came two years later, on July 26, 1956. Intense loneliness set in as Mom and Dad realized they'd be raising their children without extended family to know and love their children. They wanted to go back East. We left when I was a toddler.

We settled into the Riverside, Connecticut, home my parents would have for the next twenty-two years, complete with cocktail hour. Each evening, after my parents' self-medication, their behavior would change. Some of the time they would be happier and we could get through the evening unscathed. But sometimes it would get ugly. Their screaming at each other would awaken my brother, my sister, and me. Then they'd scream at us. Since we knew no different, we thought this was normal.

My brother, sister, and I would always ask the same question when we came home from school: "What kind of mood is Mom in?" And it usually wasn't good news. She had major personality changes that would make her fly off the handle. I hated to come home from school because I always felt she was mad at me and I didn't know why. To me, it seemed other girls went home and their mothers were always nice to them.

Luckily, I discovered ice skating when I was eight and a half years old. There were two wonderful ponds within walking distance of my house. After all the physical activity the summer provided, I craved movement in the cold of winter. I had no skates, so Mom stuffed socks into my brother's old ones. The motion of moving on the ice and the fresh air on my face felt like heaven. I'd walk there with Marcia and our neighbor friends, then escape from them on the ice. I loved the freedom I felt being out there by myself. Right away, I wanted to learn how to skate backward, so I begged my mom for lessons. My parents believed in exposing each of their children to an abundance of varied activities, in the hope they would find something they loved. They each had found a passion — Dad with his music and Mom with her horses — so it was natural for them to encourage experimentation. What none of us could possibly have known was that this new activity would take our seemingly idyllic family life and completely turn it around in just a few short years.

Mom found group lessons for me at an indoor rink in Rye, New York, in a park called Playland and signed me up. It was a thrill seeing such a massive and smooth ice surface for the first time. I couldn't wait to get on it. I had new skates, little plastic things from a discount store. I loved the lessons immediately. What I didn't like was that the lessons were only once a week, but I would spend all Thursday afternoon after the class at the public session. There was an organist playing at one end of the rink and I thought it was inspiring to skate to live music. My mom started letting me go every day and I would hang out at these public sessions. I got to know the skate guards so Mom felt comfortable dropping me off and leaving me. It was a big deal when she started letting me skate on the weekends, because that meant whole days on the ice. Each session was a couple hours long, and then the Zamboni would resurface the ice, making it clean and shiny, and I would excitedly jump on it again for another two hours. One admission would get me in for the whole day and it cost only seventy-five cents. I'd watch other skaters and was able to teach myself mohawks, three-turns, crossovers, and some spins. Barbara Taplin taught the group lessons, but she also taught privately. By the fall, after I'd turned nine, I was ready for her private lessons. At seven dollars for each half-hour lesson, I was allowed two a week. Barbara said I had to choose between swimming and skating because the two sports used muscles differently. My enthusiasm for skating made my choice clear.

Barbara was exceptional at teaching solid basics and I was fortunate she came into my life at the very beginning of my skating career. She taught the skills necessary to pass the tests regulated by the ISIA, the Ice Skating Institute of America, for recreational skaters. I was able to quickly pass their Alpha, Beta, and Gamma tests. When Playland didn't have figure-skating ice time —

we always had to compete with the hockey players for ice time — we'd go to Riverdale, where the rink had no walls. It had a roof for the commuter train to run over. Every five minutes it shook like there was a minor earthquake, but it was like paradise to me because I could skate more hours and never noticed I was freezing in the open-air rink. Back in those days, we didn't wear leggings or warm-up suits — they did not exist. We only had thin Danskin tights on our legs, material not much thicker than a pair of panty hose. There was no protection against the wind and the cold. Mom must not have liked me shivering in the cold and began taking me to an enclosed rink in Norwalk, twelve miles from our house.

There was a coach at Norwalk who intrigued me. His name was Otto Gold. He was a very proper gentleman with a German accent and a jolly smile. He taught the best skaters in the rink and he did it with a quiet strength I hadn't seen before. He seemed to me to teach a level above what I was getting from Barbara. In order to skate at this rink, I was required to join the Southern Connecticut Figure Skating Club. My parents didn't understand what that meant so Mr. Gold explained it to them. The Skating Club was a member of the United States Figure

Skating Association, the national governing body of the sport. He said the USFSA was the big leagues, not recreational; they ran all the major competitions. He advised them that I was good enough to begin working on the compulsory school figure tests of the USFSA. My parents didn't know which way to turn. They thought they had me in a satisfactory program with Barbara: It was perfect for a beginner. I made the decision for them when I looked at Mr. Gold and asked my mother, "Can I take lessons from that man?" I was nine years old.

Although I knew nothing about Mr. Gold, my instincts about his experience and abilities were correct. He had migrated from Germany to teach in Toronto and had coached Barbara Ann Scott, the first non-European to win a world championship. In 1942, she had been the first woman to land a double lutz in competition. He had also taught the legendary Canadian Don Jackson, who was the first skater to land a triple lutz in world competition when he won the world championship in 1962, receiving seven perfect marks. If nothing else, I sure as heck was going to learn a great lutz jump from him.

Mom eventually said yes to my request to take lessons from him because an incident at the Riverdale rink convinced her that I needed a change. I had overheard another coach telling Barbara Taplin that his student was better than I was and would beat me in competition. The tone he used was disturbing and I remember being very upset. It would be my first encounter with certain types of people in the figure-skating world who demonstrated their jealousy. My mother wanted to protect me from this jealous coach and switched me to the Norwalk rink and to Otto Gold. Barbara was very understanding.

What no one could have known at the time was that Mom was switching me to a completely different lifestyle. I can never thank Otto Gold enough for what he did for me. He introduced me to one of the most magical places in the world, Lake Placid, New York. This special place, in a very special time in history, would become my second home, both geographically and in my heart.

2
THE LAKE PLACID YEARS

Lake Placid, a small village with only three thousand year-round residents in the Adirondack Mountains of upstate New York, hosted the Winter Olympics in 1932 and again in 1980. I first set eyes on it in the summer of 1966. Driving up the Northway with my dad at nine years old, I had no idea what to expect as the forests became thicker and the mountains higher. The forests finally cleared and there was the town, its Main Street nestled next to the glassy blue Mirror Lake. We immediately found the rink: It was the biggest structure in town. It wasn't like any rink I had ever seen and it didn't deserve to be called a mere "rink." It was called "the Olympic Ice Arena" and had been built for the '32 Olympic Games. Double doors opened to a foyer of grand double stairs where a mammoth bronze plaque covered one wall. The plaque held the names of the gold-medal winners for every sport in the

'32 Olympics. I saw bobsled and ski jump, and then stopped when I saw figure skating. There were four names, for men, pairs, and ladies. Sonja Henie's name seemed to light up for me. I remembered my mom telling me she had had Sonja Henie paper dolls when she was a girl. I had known she must have been important, but seeing her name emblazoned there for all time, I knew I was entering into a rich sports history in a town that prided itself on bringing international winter sports competition to the United States. It would be my first summer away from the glorious and only kind of summer that I had known, the communal boat-docking with my cousins on Long Island Sound and the month spent at Rockport with my grandparents. But I didn't have a moment to miss it.

At that time, Lake Placid was the national training mecca for winter sport athletes — skiers congregated in the winter and figure skaters in the summer. I was able to be there because Otto Gold was one of the coaches who brought their students there. There was a select group of coaches from all over the world who were invited to come there when their rinks back home closed up in the summer. Otto Gold had been invited for many years and he kept a place right in the middle of town on Main Street, behind the Lake Placid Library. It was a small apartment that overlooked Mirror Lake. He and his wife, Thelma, had welcomed me to stay with them because my parents couldn't afford the infamous dorm-like McKellan's Pine Lodge, the place to stay for the out-of-town skaters. I was so happy to be in Lake Placid it didn't matter where I stayed. I had only passed one USFSA-sanctioned test, the easiest of them. It was called the Preliminary Test and any beginning skater could pass it, but Otto Gold was taking a chance on me.

I quickly discovered the joys of summer skating. It meant no school and spending all day and into the night in the rink and on the ice. We were at the rink ten hours a day. Practicing school figures took up most of our time. We were assigned patches that began each morning at 6 A.M. A patch was your own section of the ice, which measured approximately fifteen feet across and thirty feet lengthwise. The Olympic Ice Arena surface was so huge it could accommodate twenty patches in addition to the areas cordoned off for each coach. The top coaches, about seven of them in total, each had his or her own section in an L-shaped pattern down and across the ice. No one but the student taking a lesson could enter that privileged zone. Not every coach was allotted a patch and some of them shared. I was very impressed that Otto Gold had his own spot and no one else could ever use it but him.

Each patch session was forty-five minutes long, and then the ice was resurfaced and a patch would begin again. On these patches we would strive to make perfect circles, in the form of figure eights and serpentines, with nothing more than our one-eighth-inch-thick blades. It was extremely complicated and intricate. Clean edges were our goal, meaning that both the inside and outside edges could not be traced on the ice at the same time. We had to make clean three-turns, rockers, brackets, counters, and loops on our right and left inside and outside edges, both forward and backward. The figure had to be repeated over and over, practiced thousands of times, tracing the last circle we'd made with exact precision and no wobbly edges. It was a frustrating and exhausting endeavor. We needed to be good at figures because they determined at which level we could compete in the USFSA. It was always a struggle to get enough patch sessions because only twenty skaters could be on the ice at one time. There were five patch sessions in a row, every hour on the hour, and during that time it was quieter than a library, because intense concentration was required. No music was played. Coaches whispered to their students. The lights were lowered to allow as much natural light on the ice as possible, to see the tracings and patterns of our figures. Even while the ice was being resurfaced, we stayed quiet by playing cards with each other, trying to warm up our frozen fingers and toes. The loudest sound was the scratching of our scribes against the clean ice. A scribe, an instrument rather like a large protractor, was used to check the roundness of your circles or to give you a head start in practicing them by creating one to trace over.

At nine years old, I did not find this part of ice skating fun: I enjoyed free skating most because of the jumping, spinning, and speed. I worked all summer on my 1st Test and I wasn't getting any better at it. It was daunting to know there were so many tests: the Preliminary, then the 1st through 8th, which I had to pass in order to qualify to compete in Senior Ladies. Each test had more and more figures to master, and they became increasingly more difficult. The tests were taken in front of a panel of three judges who would pass or fail the skater based on a set of standards set forth by the USFSA. It was not a competition against other skaters, but an assessment of our skills. It seemed it would take a lifetime to pass these tests, as only the older teenagers were working on their 8th, also known as the Gold Test. In these early years, I thought figures were laborious and boring, and it wasn't until the last patch session was over that the rink came alive for me.

Even the locker room switched to an upbeat tone when skaters changed from their figure skates into their free-skate boots, which had stronger leather, bigger toepicks for jumping, and sharper edges. The arena was a happier place as music played, people could talk as loudly as they wanted, and skaters took to the ice in a flurry of movement. There was such a wonderful energy about the rink; even the lights were turned on brighter. First, senior skaters had the ice, the skaters who had passed certain tests. I loved to watch them because so many inspired me. Laurie Johnson was only two years older than I, but she was light on her feet and powerful at the same time: She seemed to be able to do anything. I still remember her wonderful program to Rossini's overture to *The Thieving Magpie*. There was Ellen Kinney, who could spin like a top, and I wished I could be just like her. Every girl out there could get her leg higher in a spiral than I could: I was not born very limber, but I worked constantly to be as flexible as the other girls. Then there was Gordie McKellan, whose parents owned and managed McKellan's Pine Lodge, the place that seemed to me the social center of our summer skating world. Gordie was only three years older than I, but he was already a firecracker of a skater, with smiling blue eyes, and every girl in the rink had a crush on him. I was no exception.

The Olympic Arena had stadium seating for twelve hundred people, nearly half the population of the town, and was much grander than the bleacher rinks I had skated in at home. Dotted throughout were spectators who staked out their seats each day. These were mostly the mothers of the skaters, known as the "skating moms," though not one of them ever stepped on the ice or was capable of coaching on anything about the technical side of figure skating. Most of the skaters had moms who had given up their summer to be there with their child. There were very few fathers. In fact, I don't remember any. They were all back home, working to pay for skating. My mother was not there because she still had two children who needed her care and a house to run. I didn't miss my parents or wonder if they were worried about me. My biggest concern was wanting to get my ears pierced, and I wrote them postcards begging them to allow me to do it because that was the cool thing to do. I quickly made friends with the other girls so I wouldn't be alone.

Jeannie Fortune was a local skater my age who was a lot of fun. Her family ran the Chicken Coop restaurant up the street from the arena. I lived on their delicious fried chicken in a basket, as we ate free there almost every night. When it wasn't our turn to skate, we'd walk into town and hunt through the stores. The town seemed to have one of everything — one bank, one hardware store, one dress store, and one record store — charmingly lined up on the shore of Mirror Lake, along with souvenir shops like The Trading Post. We'd stop in at Meyer's Drug Store, with its pharmacy on one side and soda fountain on the other, to get a cherry Coke. We felt so grown up. And we must have been, because no one ever kicked us out or called our parents. We walked down Main Street in our little skating dresses and Danskin tights, and all the townspeople knew we were skaters. Times have changed; we felt safe.

Many a dark night, I walked Main Street alone, getting myself back from the rink after staying late to follow the ice dancers, learning the foxtrot or the fourteen-step, and then to sit and watch the beautiful brother-and-sister pair team from Seattle, Cindy and Ron Kauffman, skate their famous program to the Beatles' "Yesterday." I would enter the Golds' apartment and smell something on their breath. It was alcohol. They seemed like different people when they drank, quick to anger and upset about the littlest things. For instance, Mrs. Gold would become livid if I did not eat the food she cooked. I usually wasn't hungry because I was full from Fortune's chicken and candy from Meyer's Drug Store (my insatiable sweet tooth). But she would make me eat because she had taken the time to prepare it. I remember her special meal of Swiss steak, so full of rich spices I was violently sick to my stomach after eating it (well, if I hadn't been so full of chicken and candy, maybe I would have kept it down).

I knew they thought they were taking good care of me, but I was doing my own thing and I don't think they understood. I turned ten midway through the summer and I invited several girls, all skaters, to my birthday party at the Golds' apartment. The mothers dropped off their girls and left, entrusting the Golds to watch over us. It was a sunny

Sunday afternoon and a bright-red water-ski jump in the middle of the four-hundred-foot-deep Mirror Lake beckoned to us. We went down to the dock on the lake to get a closer look. It was enticing. It was about ten feet high and put there for an exhibition by Wayne Grimditch, then a world champion water-ski jumper, whose family had a lovely home out on Lake Placid. We decided we would all swim out to it and jump off it. Since I had competed in swim races, it never occurred to me that some of these girls could not swim. We didn't have a single life jacket. For the younger girls, we snagged a rowboat from a nearby dock and ferried them out to the middle of the lake. We had a blast that afternoon on that red ski jump. We'd run up to the top of it, jump off into the deep mountain lake, then swim around to the bottom of the jump to do it again. The strongest swimmers helped the weaker swimmers. The Golds' golden retriever, Seawood, came out to join in the fun.

Meanwhile, one of the moms, Jessie Amelon, arrived to pick up her two daughters. Otto Gold was out and Mrs. Gold was sitting in the apartment by herself. Alarmed, she asked, "Where are the girls?"

Nonchalantly, Mrs. Gold answered, "Out on the lake."

Mrs. Amelon looked out toward the water. What a sight we must have been. Ten little girls, some as young as six, jumping off a ten-foot ski jump into four-hundred-feet-deep lake water with no life jackets.

"Get them back here!" she shouted, dashing down to the lake.

From out on the lake we saw frantic waving onshore. We piled the littlest girls back into the boat and swam the boat safely to shore. We never knew we were in danger and had defied the odds of drowning. After all, we had Seawood watching us.

Another time, Grace Vaughn, the mother of my good friend, the skater Carol Vaughn, who now manages the Rockefeller Center rink, saw us in an inner tube at one end of the lake. She couldn't call out loudly enough to make us hear, so she ran to the Golds' apartment, yelling, "Who's watching the girls?"

Mrs. Gold answered, "The dog."

Although I had little supervision, I felt very safe in Lake Placid. I was enveloped in the crisp, cool mountain air of the Adirondacks and in the definite rhythm to our days and our weeks. On Sundays the rink was closed. We would go to the beach during the day and to the movies at night, standing in line at the only theater in town. At the end of every week there was always the highlight, the Saturday night show. The historic Olympic Arena would fill with both locals and people from the neighboring towns of Saranac and North Elba. We were also the place to be on Saturday night for the tourists up from the East Coast and down from Montreal, Canada. We would prepare for our show all week long. There would be rehearsals for the group numbers, led by Cliff and Edwina Thael, a tall, graceful English couple who were also the importers for the popular John Wilson steel blades, made in Sheffield, that our sport demanded. They would choose the music, design the costumes, choreograph the numbers, and lead us in rehearsals. It was challenging to learn the footwork of the group numbers. What made it so much fun was that we were doing it together. But the coveted spots in the show were those of the soloists. The first show where I skated as a soloist, I did a belly flop stepping into a flying camel and ended up spinning on my stomach. Still, I learned to love exhibition skating in the Lake Placid shows. The spotlights were quite an adjustment for me, but soon I felt comfortable in my own little world out there. It was different from practice. Since I could not *see* the audience, perhaps I felt nobody was watching and criticizing me. I tried to get lost in the music and its mood. Eventually, I preferred it to competition skating, where the bright lights made my heart race and my legs weak.

One of the regular soloists in the Lake Placid shows was Gordie McKellan. Gordie skated every single show and often received several standing ovations. His mother, Leila, a coach, and his father, Tuffy, a former stunt skater, ran the Zamboni. After the show, we'd dress in our nicest street clothes and head over to Howard Johnson's for ice cream, then on to the Marcy Hotel on Main Street to crowd their dance floor. Firecracker Gordie never stopped being the showman. He'd get in the middle of the dance floor and spring into the air with one Russian split after another. We happily surrounded him and clapped, pushing him to do more.

Gordie's talent prompted me to take notice of his coach. He took from Gustave "Gus" Lussi. Mr. Lussi taught at the top of the L-shaped section of the ice reserved for the coaches. He had the prime spot. It was at the far end of the rink and afforded him the most privacy. No one ever invaded his space unless they had reason to be there. The *only* reason would be if you were one of his students or a parent of a student. Skaters could not choose him to be their coach. He chose his students. He was known as "the father of modern free skating" and came from Switzerland in the 1920s to teach at the Toronto Figure Skating Club, then started the first summer skating school in Lake Placid in 1932. He moved there full-time in the forties and spent winters in the Canary Islands. Lake Placid was lucky to have him in the summers. He had an international roster of students who inspired us — World and European Champion Emmerich Danzer from Austria and Toller Cranston, the creative maverick from Canada. The top U.S. skaters also gathered here because of Mr. Lussi. John Misha Petkevich came all the way from Great Falls, Montana. The hang time on his delayed Axel kept him in the air so long we thought he could jump over us.

The miracle of Mr. Lussi was that we never saw him on skates. It was rumored he wasn't a skater but a ski jumper who had mastered the physics of spinning, both in the air and on the ice. Everyone knew he had a steel plate in the front of his head from crashing on a ski jump, yet his students were the best spinners and jumpers in the rink. He taught the best sit spins in the world and he did it all standing over the boards in his privileged corner of the rink. Of course I was fascinated and intrigued.

The annual Lake Placid Open Free Skate Competition brought more skaters to the Adirondacks for a weekend in August. I wanted to be entered in the competition, which was a miracle because my first taste of competition, earlier in the spring at the Wollman Open in Central Park, was a near disaster. The mother of skaters Nancy and Bettye Wormser (who would both grow up to become well-known designers) convinced my mother I was good enough to compete and should enter the Wollman competition. Bettye graciously helped me prepare a program for it.

The biggest obstacle was having an appropriate dress for the competition. You couldn't purchase a nice dress like you can today. So skaters were at the mercy of whether or not their mothers could sew. Mom had been a field hockey player, so I was out of luck. Many of the families in skating were accustomed to having dresses made for them. Skating was an elite sport, so if the moms didn't sew, these families hired dressmakers to make custom beaded dresses. We didn't have money to spend on a dressmaker. My mom tried her best and I showed up at the Wollman competition with a dress that looked like it came from a 1920s thrift shop. All the other girls had not one, but two beautiful chiffon, beaded and embroidered dresses, one for practice and one for the competition. The outdoor Wollman Rink was melting from the spring temperatures and had inches of water on the surface. I fell in the warm-up practice and got drenched. My heavy wool dress was soaking wet, felt like it weighed fifty pounds, and stretched out uncontrollably to my knees. My tights were just as wet. We didn't know to bring along another dress and an extra set of tights. I went out to do my program and, when I did my spins, I could feel the heavy, long, wet skirt flaring out: I was like a lawn sprinkler, spraying and spitting water in a circle. It's a wonder I didn't fall over from the extra weight. I felt so embarrassed. For some reason, the judges thought I was good enough for second place. Now I see that my dress didn't matter, but boy, back then, did it ever! Like so many girls, I wanted to be Cinderella, but I felt like the ugly stepsister. I might have thought it was "all about the dress," but clearly it wasn't.

I must have been inspired by that second place, because when the anticipation of the Lake Placid Competition brought a renewed excitement to the summer, I didn't want to miss out on it. Again, I let an older skater take charge. Her name was Cynthia Van Valkenburg and she had a confident presence around the rink. She wanted a partner for the similar pairs competition, in which two girls skate side-by-side, doing the same moves. This event was not as serious as singles events. Girls paired up just for fun, but it still meant the possibility of a medal win. And it was great practice. Unfortunately, since no coach helped Cynthia and me, we tried to do it all by ourselves. We were completely unprepared when it came our turn to perform and totally blanked on our choreography.

My parents drove up to see me in this competition. I upset Mr. Gold, my parents, and myself. It appeared Cynthia and I were improvising, she calling out to me which element to do, because I couldn't remember what came next. I had also entered myself in the singles competition. When I skated the program I had choreographed myself, I was just as bad. Because of my inexperience, I had only planned the first forty seconds of it, then improvised the rest. Mr. Gold was apparently unaware of my entrance in the competition, knowing I wasn't ready for it, and he was horrified. I came in third to last. My parents felt I had wasted my summer. To make matters worse, I went back home to take the First Figure Test and failed it.

At this point I must have been so haplessly unpromising it was a wonder I didn't quit. I did poorly in school, so I wasn't happy to be back at Riverside Elementary. If I was called on in class, I would nearly black out. I'd feel my heart racing, my mouth would go impossibly dry, and I'd see stars. Today, I realize these were early signs of panic disorder. To multiply the problem, I also had learning disabilities that would probably be diagnosed today as attention deficit disorder because I couldn't focus. I was a far cry from my brilliant siblings.

My brother had been an exceptional student at this same school. His life was filled with books and studying. He'd set up the chessboard, needing a partner, and coax me to play with him, since he had mastered it himself so young. I had no idea what I was doing, but once did I beat him, by accident. It took both of us by surprise when he claimed, "That's checkmate," and had nowhere to move. I thought he was a genius scientist in the basement with his chemistry set, and he kept an Einstein poster up in his room. He was my idol (and still is) because he was so good at everything. I still fondly think of the first and only time I was better at something than Sandy. He came to the rink and rented hockey skates when I was about ten. The rink was the Crystal Ice Palace, in Norwalk, Connecticut. With birds in the rafters and rats in the popcorn, it was hardly a "palace," but it was to me . . . especially that day when Sandy came. He was a natural athlete from years of rugby and soccer, and summers as a lifeguard, yet he struggled to stand up as I whizzed past. It was the first time he was seeing me skate, and boy, did I try to show off the few jumps and spins I could do. Unfortunately, this bravado couldn't translate to the classroom. My sister was also an excellent student, a math and science brain who would go on to attain her BS in microbiology. Surely the teachers at Riverside Elementary had assumed I would do well because brains are supposed to run in families. When I came along, the runt in the family, they must have been disappointed, but I wish they had known I didn't panic because I didn't know the answer. I panicked because I was so incredibly nervous. No way was I going to talk in front of a group of people.

But I never felt that way out on the ice — well, at least not during practice. I let movement do my talking for me. It was how I could express myself. I wanted so much to improve after getting a big-league taste of figure skating during my wonderful summer. I just didn't know how to do it. Passion is one thing, but hard work is another, and I didn't know the value of working hard. My mom was an efficient taskmaster. She didn't want to see me frittering away my time and their hard-earned money. She demanded that I work hard at skating or not do it at all. That was my choice. I didn't want to give it up, so I had no option but to learn how to work hard.

Clearly, my mom realized she couldn't just drop me off and trust others, even a coach as respected as Otto Gold, to see that I worked hard. She stuck around. She was suddenly thrust into the role of a skating mom. But she was different from the other mothers. She sat off by herself and pretended to read a book while she was really watching me. One mom who got to know her said she had been reading the same book upside down all winter. I always knew she was watching me and so I couldn't keep up my socializing by the side of the boards: She glared at me if I tried to start up conversations during a practice session. She also glared at other skaters if they tried to talk to me. Every second of ice time became precious, and her presence was a constant reminder that I was lucky to get it. We began to get up at five thirty in the morning to skate before school just so I could get in two more valuable patch sessions. More rinks were added to our repertoire as we chased down ice time. I'd get out of school at two thirty and we'd race to either Rye or Norwalk or New Haven or Hartford or into New Jersey to the studio rink owned by Fritz Dietle, who was the stilt skater in the professional ice shows. His rink was very small, only the size of eight patches, but if it provided ice time, we were there. My mom was endlessly creative in her quest for more ice time, but sometimes she was up against a brick wall — like when she went to my principal to ask if I could get excused from gym class so that I could practice more before school. I was now in the fifth grade.

The principal asked, "Can't she just do it in the afternoon, like the swimmers do?"

My mom explained that I already did skate in the afternoon but more ice time was necessary for training in figures. She tried to make him understand the unending quest for patch sessions. She argued that because I was already getting so much physical activity outside of school, I really didn't need gym class. But there was no convincing him. He had no clue what it took to train as a figure skater and she was refused.

But she knew not to push it any further. She saw my skating as a back-up to my education and put academics first. She worried that if I got hurt or lost interest, I wouldn't have anything to fall back on. I don't think she ever imagined that her little girl could win the Olympics and get a contract with Ice Capades. That scenario would have been more difficult for her to envision than finding a needle in a haystack. At most, she hoped I might become good enough to coach other skaters. And all I wanted was to become a better skater. I was so young and so focused, I couldn't begin to appreciate the battles my mother fought for me, and her endless sacrifices. Sometimes when I think of all she did, even today, it brings tears to my eyes.

I continued to take lessons from Otto Gold and finally passed the 1st Test. But I kept thinking about Gus Lussi. I asked the same question of my mother as I did earlier when I referred to Otto Gold, but this time I had Gus Lussi on my mind: "Can I take lessons from that man?"

The second summer, I went up to Lake Placid more prepared. Dad stayed with Marcia, and Sandy went to my grandparents' house so that Mom could come up with me. She was able to rent a two-bedroom apartment above the garage of the Fortunes' "camp" out on Lake Placid. The lake called Lake Placid was adjacent to the town bearing its name and only had residential development along its shores. The "Adirondack Camp," built from local timber and stone, was an architectural style made famous by wealthy industrialists before the Depression. These camps were larger than most homes. The Fortunes' camp was up a private drive called Humdinger Hill: There were a mere ten camps on this road and it was very secluded. We took in two boarders, the skaters Don Bonacci and Lee Meadows, to help pay our rent. Their share of the rent made my summer skating possible, and my mom was responsible for driving them to the rink, now several miles away. They shared one bedroom while my mom and I shared the other. There was a big kitchen where we spent evenings playing cards, which was much safer than my trolling Main Street. From the garage, we could walk straight down the hill and take a swim in the lake. The view was magical. The lake was huge, with three large islands. Overlooking the lake was the majestic Whiteface Mountain, the second highest peak in the region. A happy Sunday excursion would be driving to the top of it and taking in the view of the Adirondacks. But my happiest memories of this summer were my lessons with Gus Lussi.

I was fortunate to have Mr. Lussi take me on. It was as if I had entered the inner sanctum of an exclusive club when I became one of his students. He chose students as much for their talent as for their passion for skating. I now had access to his private section of the arena and to his other students. I loved that he demanded so much of me because it made me want to work harder to please him. He was strict about warming up. Before we were allowed to start jumping, we had to stroke around the ice for a full ten minutes, long glides forward and backward, and do only spins until sweat was pouring off of us. He didn't teach me any jumps for our first two weeks together. He said if a skater couldn't spin correctly on the ice, they wouldn't be able to do it in the air. I came to understand his technique so well on only two lessons a week that I taught myself a double toe loop. He found so many ways to inspire his students because he relished our love of skating and he loved skaters who appreciated other skaters. He encouraged us to watch and listen to him teach his other students. From his corner of the boards, he arranged friendly competitions among his students. Mr. Lussi pitted me against his finest and believed I could be strong enough to keep up with the male jumpers. Suddenly, I found myself in a fun showdown with the skater I had so admired from last summer, and the boy on whom I would always have a crush, Gordie McKellan. We would take turns doing delayed Axels and measure who could jump the farthest. Gordie would go on to become our national champion a year before I did, in 1973, so he was the perfect incentive for me to fly farther.

Mr. Lussi was as concerned about our conduct and character as he was about our skating. He expected us to be ladies and gentlemen at all times. He demanded proper manners and that we show respect for the other skaters. He was never mean, never put anyone down or gave false encouragement. He would never tell us we had done something poorly. If he got frustrated with us, he never showed it. He would shake his head, turn, walk away from the boards, and take a moment before he came back to say, "Let's try it again." When we did something right, he would say, "Now that's what I'm talking about." He was also concerned about presentation and was a confidence builder. As a young child, I was so meek that if someone asked my name I'd run away. He wouldn't let me get away with that.

"What is your name?" he'd ask me.

"Dorothy," I'd say, barely above a whisper.

"Dorothy who?" he'd ask.

"Dorothy Hamill," I'd answer, still so softly.

"What is your name?" he'd ask again, louder.

"Dorothy Hamill," I'd say, trying to match his tone.

"WHAT IS YOUR NAME?" He wouldn't let up until I said it with self-confidence.

"DOROTHY HAMILL," I finally declared, standing taller.

Dick Button, the two-time Olympic men's champion and one of Lussi's most famous former students, would come to town and visit. He would walk the length of the arena and we all knew where he was headed: to Gus Lussi's patch of ice, to watch the next prodigy Mr. Lussi had discovered. Mr. Lussi invited others in his inner sanctum to listen in on lessons. He encouraged the parents to do so. But my mom, of course, had to be different.

My mom would sit up high in the bleachers, not wanting to disturb us. She'd had a nice life before she was forced into sitting in ice rinks. She'd bowled, had bridge parties, and took French. She wasn't like the other skating moms. She didn't like their gossipy natures, kept to herself, and made only a few friends. The friends she made truly treasured her. One of her friends was Grace Vaughn and it was a relief for me when Grace would coax Mom out of the rink to go for coffee at Howard Johnson's. There were always skaters better than I, and Mom's glares from high in the seats would let me know she knew that. She made me feel that nothing I did was good enough for her. For instance, it took me a while to master a double flip, a milestone for a figure skater because the take-off was from a more difficult turn than anything we'd already learned. I finally landed one when I was eleven. I raced over to the boards, hoping for praise from Mom. I have a people-pleaser personality: Most of all I wanted to please my mom.

Instead, she said, "Those other girls are jumping higher."

She had no idea how crushed I was. I was too immature to understand my hurt or to know how to get positive feedback from her. When my father drove up on weekends, it was a relief for both my mom and me because we had a break from each other. Without hesitation, he jumped into the action of the rink, and loved standing next to Mr. Lussi for my lessons.

With a huge smile on his face, Dad would

take in everything Mr. Lussi had to say and delight in my enthusiastic progress. By then, Dad had begun to take a more active role in my skating. He wanted to do all he could, besides just paying the bills. He learned how to sharpen my blades just the way I loved them. He loved to take the time to polish my skates, making them look perfect. He even ironed my laces. And he washed the little white gloves we were expected to wear for doing figures in tests and competitions. After closely observing my lessons, my dad was able to recap them. He made a fun game of repeating a lesson to me. It was invaluable to me to hear the instructions given to me again. Even though my mother had sat and watched the lessons all summer, and probably knew every instruction by heart, I didn't want to hear them from her. Although she didn't repeat them meanly, I felt that her tone was critical of me. Somehow, when the same words came out of my father's mouth, I was inspired and wanted to please him. But I didn't dwell on what my mother thought of me because I cared most deeply about how Mr. Lussi felt. Soon, I received the greatest compliment he gave to his skaters. It was the best day of the summer when he called me over to demonstrate a sit spin to one of his other students. I knew then that I had mastered a sit spin in the eyes of the one who counted most, Mr. Lussi.

That summer, I was determined to be ready for the Lake Placid Free Skate Competition. I was entered in Juvenile Ladies: This category was for the young beginning skaters who had passed the Preliminary and 1st USFSA Tests. Even though I didn't have a pretty embroidered chiffon dress like the other competitors arriving from all over the East Coast, I knew I had worked hard and hoped I would do better than I had the past summer.

My dad drove up again for the competition and he could tell I was very nervous. He was successful in calming my nerves by diverting my attention before I went out to skate. My parents knew how much I still wanted to get my ears pierced. I'd been bugging them every day because Cindy Kauffman, the beautiful pairs skater from Seattle, was icing up skaters' ears and putting needles in them herself.

Shortly before I went out to skate, I asked my parents, "If I win first place, can I have my ears pierced?"

Probably thinking I didn't have a chance at winning, they said, "Yes."

"Really?"

"But you have to get it done at the doctor's office."

I was so excited, but then I thought a minute and I said, "What if I come in second place?"

"You can have one ear pierced," Dad said. I laughed.

"What if I come in third place?"

"You can have your nose pierced," Dad said.

The announcer called my name and I stepped out on the ice, laughing from the joke. I skated my best and won first place. I had gone from embarrassing myself to being a winner in just one year.

My parents kept their promise. We went to the town doctor, Dr. Hart. His office on Main Street was right next to the Chicken Coop restaurant. He charged us twelve dollars and I paid for it from money I had saved from Jonsie and Bill's birthday gift.

The culmination of every Lake Placid season of summer skating for generations had been the Labor Day Show. A theme would be chosen, and fresh group numbers were created by the Thaels. A whirl of rehearsals kept us busy every afternoon for weeks. We performed the same show four times over a busy tourist weekend. It was a caliber above the Saturday night shows, almost on the level of a professional ice show. Champions would be invited to skate, and they would fly in from all over the country.

Janet Lynn arrived from the Wagon Wheel Figure Skating Club in Rockford, Illinois, and I was mesmerized by her athletic energy, grace, and flow across the ice. Most of all, I was entranced by the obvious joy she felt as she skated. Her eyes and her smile lit up the rink like a beam of light and everyone loved her. My mother had been after me to look as if I was enjoying myself during a performance. I thought I was enjoying myself and I was tired of her bugging me about it. I thought I might look silly smiling. Then I saw Janet Lynn skate. She looked like an angel. I was so captivated I thought I would try to emulate her. I found I skated better when I smiled and I even enjoyed performing more. Why not share the happiness I felt while I was skating? I loved it so much it got to a point where I didn't like skating to music where it was inappropriate to show joy. There are always skaters who make a connection to that joy without smiling. I am not one of them. Peggy Fleming, with her elegance and regal quality, was one of them. Audiences were captivated just by her movement.

And thank goodness for Peggy Fleming. She was going to lead a new generation to save American figure skating . . .

Our beloved sport had been shattered to its core only a few years earlier by a catastrophic event that loomed over us like a dark cloud. The skaters, coaches, officials, judges, and parents of our generation were deeply impacted by the 1961 plane crash in Belgium that killed our U.S. figure skating team, along with their coaches, families, and skating officials. In all, seventy-two people had perished on Sabena flight 548 leaving New York and bound for the world championships in Prague, Czechoslovakia. Worlds were canceled that year. The crash wiped out a generation of American figure skating and obliterated all hope for U.S. medal wins in the next Olympics, as these were the skaters being groomed to represent our country. Laurence Owen was only sixteen when she died on this flight. She had placed fifth the year before at the Squaw Valley Olympics, her first year of international competition, and she was slated to rise to Olympic gold in the 1964 Innsbruck Olympics. Her mother, Maribel Vinson-Owen, the nine-time U.S. ladies' champion, and her sister, also named Maribel and on the world team as a pairs skater, were also killed. Maribel Vinson-Owen had coached Tenley Albright to the first Olympic gold medal for an American in ladies' figure skating and proudly coached both her own daughters. Maribel had won a silver medal in the 1932 Olympic Games in Lake Placid. Her name was on the mammoth bronze plaque that dominated the Olympic Arena entrance and was our daily reminder of figure skating's loss.

The crash impacted all of America because, for the first time that year, the U.S. championships had been broadcast on national television. America came to know the world team members who would represent them overseas and fell in love with them. Then, just two weeks later, they were all dead. It was impossible to fathom.

There would be no gold for the American skaters in the 1964 Innsbruck Olympics. Our new team was too young and inexperienced in international competition. U.S. skating had to start all over again. The president of the USFSA, F. Ritter Shumway, established the USFSA Memorial Fund just two months after the crash, to jump-start a new generation of skaters, but it wasn't enough to compete with the Communist bloc countries of East Germany and the USSR. They quickly dominated international figure skating because their governments fully subsidized them. It created a double standard, since American skaters, as amateur athletes, had to pay their own way.

It cost at least twenty thousand dollars a year at that time to compete. Coaching, ice time, choreography, music, travel, costumes, skates, and blades were just the beginning of a skater's expenses. Skating competitively also often meant establishing a second home near qualified coaches. No wonder the Memorial Fund made little impact.

It was up to the new generation to rebuild, and we carried the burden on our small, pre-pubescent shoulders. Fortunately, we were led by a beautiful young woman who changed the face of American skating with her unique grace, and in the summer of 1967, we were lucky to have her skate in the Lake Placid Labor Day Show. Peggy Fleming flew in from the Broadmoor Figure Skating Club in Colorado Springs to perform her program to "What's New Pussycat?" — a fitting piece of music, since she represented all that was new and blazed trails for us. Unfortunately, we also had a wake-up call over this Labor Day weekend, the last weekend of the big summer. Gary Visconti, our men's national champion, had been invited to skate in the Labor Day Show. He came from Detroit with his coach, Don Stewart. Between each of the skaters there was always a "spotlights going out" blackout during which the applause would calm down from the previous skater and the next skater's name would be announced. During this blackout, the next skater would appear from around the curtain and stroke around the ice in darkness. When Gary took to the ice, he could not stand up. He kept falling. It was as if he had tennis shoes on his feet, not skates with blades. He could not get a grip on the ice. So many of us were lined up beside the curtain to watch our hero skate. Instead, we watched in horror as he fell again and again. When they announced his name and the lights came up, he shook his head and walked off the ice.

Don Stewart immediately ran to Gary's side. He took a quick look at Gary's blades and knew what was wrong. Gary had had his blades sharpened earlier that afternoon and had left his skates unattended on the bench in the men's locker room before the show. During that time, someone had tampered with his blades. In a stellar, decade-long skating career that had taken him around the globe, it had never occurred to him to worry that anyone would harm him. We were aghast. We never did learn who could have done such a horrible thing, but we did learn a big lesson that day. Although America was staking a new claim on the international stage, it was first and foremost a fiercely competitive, individual sport. I vowed I would never leave my skates unattended, but as I would later learn, that would not be enough protection in a world where your best friend might be your rival. Gary went on to become an Olympic team member alongside Peggy Fleming in 1968, but he never did find out who wanted to hurt him that day.

The glorious summer ended and we went home to Riverside. The highlight of coming home was seeing my best friend, Kim Danks. We had met before I started skating, and we bonded over listening to the Beatles' music and playing with our Barbie dolls. Kim was the oldest of four and let me try out her roller skates. I loved the speed and the movement, but not the noise and weight of the rollers. When I started ice skating, our days of walking home from school together and hanging out on the front stoop of Aida's, the penny-candy store, were over. Even though we hadn't seen each other all summer, weekly postcards helped, and when I gave her a call, it was as if we had never been out of touch.

Still, I couldn't see her very often because I had to return to a practice regimen that meant traveling to five different rinks in a week. It felt depressing not to have the inspiration of Mr. Lussi for the winter. Since he'd gone to the Canary Islands, I was without a coach. My mom was determined to make the best of the forced change. She became convinced that I needed a female coach because people told her I wasn't graceful enough. It was assumed in the skating world that a woman was more capable of teaching graceful movements to a girl than a man was. My father deferred to my mother on all the major decisions regarding my skating. There was no way I was ever going to be a beautiful swan like Peggy Fleming, but Mom seemed so strong and sure of herself, and I was much too young to make these decisions for myself. My mother is a tall woman, much bigger than the woman I would grow to be, with an even larger personality. Although she did not intend it, she was intimidating to me — and to others, as I would later learn. Little did I know that she was not sure of herself at all. She just went with her instincts. She hadn't raised a figure skater before and she didn't have a clue what she was doing. She wished my dad would take more responsibility for these decisions, but he couldn't. He was too busy working and paying the bills. It was my mother who stayed up nights worrying about what to do. To my mom's credit, her sleepless nights were worth it. Her next move was brilliant.

3
Bright Lights, Big City Girl

One of the rinks where I practiced was the Skating Club of New York, which at that time was on the third floor of the original Madison Square Garden. The Skating Club of New York had a storied history. It was the second-oldest figure-skating club in the United States, having been founded in 1863. Its original home was a pond across from the Plaza Hotel on the edge of Central Park. During the 1930s, the club produced the lavish ice extravaganzas at Madison Square Garden, headlined by Sonja Henie. The Skating Club of Boston, the Philadelphia Skating Club and Humane Society, and the Skating Club of New York were the founding members of the USFSA. Meetings were held in the homes of the members. They established a national championship based on the tradition of the club's Middle Atlantic championships. For the next thirty years, the skaters from the Skating Club of New York dominated national and international competition. After World War II and the reign of Dick Button, the sport became more popular, and skating clubs began to spring up all over the country.

Among the Skating Club of New York's Olympians were Beatrix Loughran, Sherwin Badger, Carol Heiss, and Sonya Klopfer. My mom began talking to my father and me about Sonya. Sonya had married another coach named Peter Dunfield and they coached together at SCNY.

I first knew of Sonya Dunfield when I competed in the Skating Club's Middle Atlantic Competition. She had the star students of the time, like Valerie Levine and Terri Cheeseman. I had fun at the rink with these girls. We'd go into the bathroom during breaks, make spitballs out of paper towels, and throw them out the window, watching them hit the sidewalk three floors below. They were my age, yet they were much better skaters than I was. I had become the most advanced at Playland and there was no one to look up to. I had learned from Gus Lussi how important it was to learn by example and appreciate the work of other skaters. I loved being here with these fantastic girls. I felt so welcomed by my competitors.

Dad started driving me into New York City on weekends to skate, while during the week I still had ice time at Playland. It was a one-hour drive, and Dad drove in both Saturday and Sunday. I loved my weekends with him. On these drives we would talk about skaters we loved, but most of all, we'd listen to music and discuss our favorite songs and the feelings they evoked. He'd edit together music he thought I should use for my programs. It was always music way too strong for me, but he could only envision me as the strong skater I wanted to become. Mr. Lussi wanted me to see that I could be strong, gutsy, tough, and ladylike all at the same time. My dad understood that and also realized that I wanted to skate this way. He appreciated my athleticism and felt music like Tchaikovsky's *Romeo and Juliet* would express it. My father saw the future Dorothy before I could ever see her. I later grew into these strong pieces — well, maybe not completely — but it was something to shoot for.

My skating days were so different when Dad was around. He would park the car and carry my skates into the rink for me, whereas Mom would drop me off and shoo me into the rink. He was very meticulous about the care of my skates and made sure he dried the blades with a chamois, instead of a terry-cloth towel. He always had a handkerchief ready for my runny nose. He would stay all day at the rink and watch me. I'd do three hours of patch and two hours of free skating each day. People responded happily to his friendly, always smiling demeanor and we felt well-liked. The exciting talk around the rink was the building of the new home for the SCNY. It was going to be called the Skyrink because it was being built on the six-teenth floor of an office building on Thirty-third Street between Tenth and Eleventh Avenues.

Sonya was energetic and enthusiastic, and loved to chat. And, boy, did she talk fast! It was enough for me to keep up with her. Although she would soon be elected into the Figure Skating Hall of Fame, she was still young enough to demonstrate for her skaters. She showed us Axels, Wally jumps, and spirals, and always had the most beautiful camel spin in the rink. All my coaches had been on me about my terrible posture and arm movements, but now, watching Sonya's pretty upright posture, I finally understood the importance of a straight back. I began emulating her. Her husband, Peter, was an articulate disciplinarian from Canada, who was well known as a pairs coach from his work with the great U.S. pairs team, Mark and Melissa Militano. He had a gift for the business side of skating, but also for choosing music and putting together choreography for a program. Together, they made an indominitable pair.

That year, 1968, my Christmas present from my parents was a trip to Philadelphia to watch Peggy Fleming, Janet Lynn, and John Misha Petkevitch compete in Nationals. They were held in the new, spectacular Spectrum arena, and the competition would determine the members of the Olympic team in Grenoble. I remember sitting next to John Misha's uncle, who was so nervous for his nephew that he tightly held onto his rosary beads under his coat as Misha competed. Janet Lynn attempted a triple Salchow, the first time a woman tried it in American competition. She didn't land it, but she took skating to a new level by trying it. Peggy Fleming's grace and elegance won. There was a renewed sense of hope in the air, a feeling that the American figure skating world was finally free of the black cloud that had hung over it since the '61 crash. I was so inspired watching the events, I went home and worked even harder than before.

I began to pass the figure tests necessary to compete at a national level. I passed my 2nd, then my 3rd. I needed my 4th and 5th to compete in Novice Ladies. The other girls had the advantage of skating several hours in the morning before school, while I was only skating a half hour. My mother had put 100,000 miles on her car in just one year and my dad drove a beat-up Volkswagen Beetle to make ends meet, yet when I asked to skate more hours before school they miraculously did not balk.

Suddenly, my mom and I had a more grueling schedule. We woke at 4 A.M. to get into New York and on the ice by five fifteen. I would skate until seven forty-five; my only break was changing into my free skating boots after finishing two patch sessions. My mom would speed me back to Connecticut to school, to arrive at eight thirty-five, and then go to work. She had taken a job at a nursery school to help pay for my skating. I'd be released at two thirty from what I perceived as my prison, because I was such a horrible student. Mom would race me off to Rye or Norwalk or Riverdale or New Haven or Hartford or New Jersey to skate until past dinnertime. We'd come home to a house uncared for, because my mom had been gone for fourteen hours. She then worked into the night on laundry, dishes, and housecleaning. It was much tougher on her than it was on me. After all, I was doing what I loved. She made it clear that she was doing this for me because it was my choice. She was the antithesis of some other skating moms we'd met who pushed their daughters to be the stars their moms never were.

She'd say to me, "You want this, Dorothy. I don't." And it would make me want it more. And I wanted it really badly. One early morning when I was around this age, when Mom didn't get up in time to drive me to the rink, I started walking there myself. Fortunately, my sister alerted Mom that I was gone and she came after me. By the time her car stopped to pick me up, I was about a mile up the road.

But my drive would also make me feel guilty and selfish. I felt I was some kind of spoiled brat. I knew that the arguments about money, for instance, the constant reminding to turn off lights to save on electric bills, were the result of the money spent on my skating. But we weren't spending nearly the amount that other skating families were spending. We couldn't afford choreography because it meant more lessons from a coach. So I did my own choreography. Combined with not having the same quality of dresses as the other girls, I felt self-conscious, ugly, stupid, and unsophisticated in their presence. The only way to compensate was to be a better skater. And the only way to be a better skater was to work harder.

My mom would never demean another skater. She spoke glowingly of them, appreciating them. But, not understanding, I took those comments as criticisms of my own skating. It seemed as if she was reinforcing my own belief that I was not good enough. Everyone else was better than I was. Nothing I ever did was good enough for her. But I was too young and too wrapped up in my own world to see how much she was being pulled in so many directions. She had three children to care for, a home that constantly needed attention, and a husband who worked nonstop to pay the bills, leaving him no time to help her with the daily chores of housework. This situation would be daunting for any woman, but my mom also had the burden of managing an obsessed young figure skater. She had no idea how to do it. She was totally unprepared and caught by surprise. Yet so much was expected of her. I didn't know it at the time, but my mother suffered from bouts of depression that also afflicted her family, and these stressful pressures added to her misery. Her brother, my Uncle Dave, had been outspoken about his depression, and the depression that runs in the family, while my mother remained silent. But their depression wasn't diagnosed until my siblings and I were well into adulthood. I feel so awful about it now, words cannot describe it. If I had known, if she had known, we all could have understood it at the time and would have felt empathy for her. Instead, I felt a growing anger toward her inability to accept me. But I was forced to repress it if I was to continue skating. She was my only lifeline to the sport. If I had caused trouble with her, I knew she would have stopped sacrificing her life for the thing that made me happy. Sometimes I felt so forgiving toward my mom and other times I felt just the opposite. I was so conflicted about my feelings toward her that, even to this day, I still struggle to find understanding.

My mother was a fairly volatile person, but the source of our conflict did not rest solely on her shoulders. My parents were a well-matched pair in many ways, and I was lucky I inherited athletic talent and musicality from them. But they were also dangerous for each other. Depression also lurked in the shadows on my father's side. His younger brother, my Uncle Jim, had committed suicide. Depressed persons of his generation didn't understand what was wrong with them. If they did come forward and admit to depression, the medical profession would conveniently put them away in an institution. The pharmaceuticals that now help the chemical imbalances of millions didn't exist in those days. Psychological issues were seen as a character flaw, a mental weakness that could be overcome by sheer will or complete denial. People felt shame and didn't come forward with their problems.

My father's smiling demeanor hid his depression. He had found his happiness early in life in the world of music, but was unable to pursue it because of family pressures. Dad felt obligated to his parents, whose high expectations made him feel less than successful (sound familiar?). They dismissed his artistic ambitions and expected him to be responsible in a stable profession. Getting out from under their demands didn't set him free, because soon he was obligated to my mother and to us. When I look back, I feel sorry for my dad and the daily grind of a job that didn't satisfy his creative yearnings. He'd come home from work, and my parents would have their cocktails to get through the night. This behavior had more serious consequences for me after I started skating.

Because I had to rise so early, I'd always go to bed early. But, on occasion, the sleep would not last long. When my parents' voices would elevate and tempers got short, yelling would ensue. Marcia would come into my room and comfort me. We heard their loud swearing. My mom and dad almost never used foul language unless they were arguing, and though I could only guess what the rest of the screaming words were, I was positive it was all my fault. I assume it was about the lack of money and the piling on of endless, impossible responsibilities no one person could handle, let alone a women suffering from depression. At least my father could get away from the doldrums of domestic responsibility by going to work. And he worked all the time.

My saddest and earliest memory, from when I was three or four, is of our priest coming over to our house to convince my mother not to leave my father. She had gone to the train station and bought tickets, then she had packed up her children to take to my grandmother's house. She wanted a divorce. She was a modern woman trapped in the era of fifties' moms, who were expected to be invisible, be of constant service to their family, and have no voice. The priest convinced her it was her duty to stay with my father.

There was no way Sandy, Marcia, and I could be compassionate enough to have any kind of understanding of what my parents were going through, particularly my mother. What could she do? A child can only internalize parental anger. I interpreted their fights as "I must have done something wrong." I shook in my bed, too frightened to cry. It was a time when people weren't allowed to voice their feelings because it would appear that they were wallowing in them. And I wasn't about to wallow in mine. I just had a feeling nothing would ever be good enough for my mother. My mother always seemed to be unhappy with me, whether she was drinking or not.

My brother, Sandy, eventually escaped our home by getting a scholarship to Phillips Exeter Academy, a boarding prep school, at the tender age of twelve. Sandy and my father had a very acrimonious relationship: I remember that their fights were loud and frequent. My dad demanded perfection and he was toughest on his only son, just as his parents had been toughest on him. He'd insist, "If you can't do it right, don't bother doing it at all." He expected us to be the best at whatever we chose to do. Even if we tried basket weaving, we'd better be the best damn basket weaver the world had ever seen. My brother was better off leaving the pressure cooker we called home. His gifted ability, combined with our stark financial picture, earned him both scholarships *and* freedom. That left Marcia and me to fend against our parents.

The bottom line was that both my parents went undiagnosed and untreated for depression. Using alcohol was the way they could medicate themselves and deal with the normal ups and downs of everyday life. What they wouldn't know was that their children stood a great chance of inheriting the gene for depression. Since my parents' generation didn't understand the disease, it would be left to our ill-equipped generation to wrangle with its mysterious effects after we grew up.

No wonder I escaped to the happiness I found at the rink as a child. My parents could have made me quit to make their lives manageable, but they never brought up the subject. My grandmother Jonsie noticed the stress on our family and suggested we should "take a year off."

"You don't understand," my mom answered. "A year off means the end."

Good thing she didn't listen to Jonsie, because the next year would transform me.

I adored my coach, Sonya Dunfield. Her constantly optimistic nature was, for me, a necessary contrast to my mother's negativity. My mother continued to be contrary about everything with me. If I said something was white, she'd disagree and say it was black. Sonya was the opposite, always pushing me forward and upward, especially on my compulsory figures. Most of my technique in free skating was from Gus Lussi. My parents and I didn't know at the time, because we didn't know any better, but he was not as adept at teaching figures as he was at free skating. He taught using unorthodox methods that puzzled me for years. Sonya was the first to be able to break down bad habits I was forming. With her guidance, I was able to pass my 4th Test and qualify for Novice Ladies. I didn't do very well that year because the other girls were so much older and more experienced than I was, but I felt a great deal of satisfaction in my progress because I was competing in a division, although it was the lowest, that could qualify for Nationals.

I arrived that summer in Lake Placid ready to have the same great experiences I had had the previous summer. I was especially looking forward to more free skating lessons with Mr. Lussi (not so with figures!). His games made free skating fun and challenging. He had a game called "Add-On." A skater would do a jump; the next skater would do that jump and add on another jump; and the next skater would do the first two jumps and add their own. This would go on until there was a sequence of so many jumps that it was a challenge not only to complete the jumps but just to remember their order. Whoever fell or couldn't complete the series of jumps was out of the game. This game was great training to land the jumps no matter what!

My mother and I rented the same apartment above the Fortunes' garage with the same enthusiasm we'd had the summer before. But something had changed with my Novice Ladies standing, something I didn't expect. Some parents now considered me a threat to some of the other girls. I didn't realize at the time why I was being treated differently. Leila McKellan let my mother know that there was one family conspiring to sabotage me. The girl and her mother had signed up for many more lessons from Mr. Lussi than my family could possibly afford. Mr. Lussi had now gone up to twenty dollars per twenty-minute lesson. He could charge so much because he was in high demand. He made enough in the summertime to provide him with those precious winters in the Canary Islands. He was so world-renowned and so much in high demand that he could name his price and people would pay it.

That my new competitor was manipulating Lussi's schedule was disheartening, but that was only part of it. Her parents insisted to Mr. Lussi that I not be asked to give any demonstrations for her or play Add-On with her, as that would disturb her. Since my parents could not book all my lessons with Mr. Lussi, I began taking them from other coaches. I took lessons from Mary Batdorf very early in her career. She was only twenty years old. Mary and her twin sister, Anne, were protégées of Gus Lussi. Mary would go on to teach many champions, including Nancy Kerrigan. Lussi did not mind if his students took lessons from any other coach in the arena except for one. It was forbidden to take lessons from the British coach Howard "Nick" Nicholson and Gus Lussi at the same time. Gus wouldn't allow it. They were both exceptional coaches and their ongoing friction had begun long before any of us were born. Nobody knew what had caused the friction and it was the mystery of the rink. Nick was the coach I needed most that summer because he was known for teaching compulsory figures. His skaters had the best figures not only in the rink but also in the world. Nick loved to teach figures and Gus loved to teach free skating. It seemed so silly that they couldn't work together, since Gus hated teaching figures as much as Nick disliked teaching free skating!

People would lavish Mr. Lussi with expensive gifts to gain his favor. My family couldn't compete on that level. But that summer, Gus gave me a lasting gift that was priceless. As a side business and just for fun, he owned a successful restaurant, aptly named "Lussi's." It had a Bavarian theme and three ponds from which customers could catch their own fish, to be prepared by the chef for their dinner. Mr. Lussi loved all things Swiss and suggested I skate to the song "Edelweiss." He gave me a dried Edelweiss flower that I cherish to this day. I idolized Julie Andrews and imagined myself being Maria in *The Sound of Music*.

I was progressing somewhat rapidly. I was now in the free skate sessions with the top skaters. Once, Emmerich Danzer accidentally sliced my right leg open so deep that when I reached down to pull my torn tights up, my entire fingernail slipped inside the wound. My dad was there and he rushed me to Dr. Hart to get stitches. While I was at the doctor's office, someone stole my father's brand-new movie camera. My dad loved to film my skating to document my progress.

When I returned home in the fall, I began to take the train back from New York by myself. I was only twelve years old. Today, a parent wouldn't dare let a little girl travel alone in the city, but back then we were naïve, because the world seemed free of the dangers that frighten us today. So, for a while at least, my mother and I had a nice break from each other. She could stay at home to be a parent to Marcia and a wife to my father. My brother was now a senior boarder at Exeter. This arrangement didn't last long because my competitions were coming up quickly — the regional competition is always held in December. My region was North Atlantics.

There are nine regional competitions held throughout the United States. Any skater is eligible to compete, as long as he or she has passed the USFSA-sanctioned figure tests for their division. As many as thirty skaters can compete in one division in the first part of the competition, which, back then, were figures. Only the top nine skaters in figures were eligible to do the free skate. This was now my second year in Novice, but we still had little hope that I would be in the top nine. At the last minute, my mom packed an extra dress I could wear for the free skate, just in case.

I surprised everyone, most of all myself, by placing in the top nine after the figures, then skating well enough to move up to third place in the free skate, barely winning the last spot to qualify for Easterns. Only nine skaters make it to Easterns in each division, three from each Regional competition. The top three from each division are sent to Nationals. I had no expectation that I would go to Nationals, as I had somehow slipped into this last spot. That meant eight girls were potentially better than I.

Thankfully, I was gaining confidence because the Dunfields believed in me. They breathed new life into my attitude and made me want to work harder. We continued to add more difficulty to my free skate program as we edged toward Easterns. We also worked hard to improve my awkward arm movements and choppy skating strokes. Most skaters kept their program the same throughout the season because the competitions were so close together — Regionals in December, Sectionals in January, and Nationals in February. Making changes took a lot of time to perfect. It was risky for me to change mine, but frankly I was still such a neophyte I didn't know any better. I felt I was improving and I wanted to show it. It paid off in a big way. I came in third at Easterns, qualifying for Nationals! Everyone was surprised, but no one more than I. Back at the Skating Club of New York, local judges pushed me to take my 5th Test because then my figures would be stronger for Nationals. After my initial failing of the 1st Test, I had now passed six of the eight USFSA-sanctioned tests in only two years. All in all, passing the figure tests that quickly was amazing, but at the same time, it made me the weakest in the "advanced" category. Meanwhile, in free skating, I continued to improve and added a double lutz to my program.

Suddenly I was on my way to the Seattle Nationals in February, representing the Eastern United States in Novice Ladies. Again, there would only be nine girls qualifying, three from Easterns, three from Midwesterns, and three from Pacific Coast. Again, that meant eight girls were potentially better than I. Qualifying for the U.S. Nationals was the big time. Wow! I was so excited I couldn't wait to experience the highest level in the United States. The year was 1969. The flight to Seattle was my first time on an airplane. I flew with Sonya, and when we arrived, we went shopping to find gloves to go with my figure dress. I have always loved the costume side of figure skating, even though, at this age, I was very limited in what I could do because our financial resources were scarce. Sonya had found someone to help my mom make my competition dresses: It was evident Mom could not do it on her own. The dresses were still very plain, not beaded and sparkling like the other girls'. Plain isn't a bad thing, but a skating dress does need to fit, and these didn't flatter my movement because of their poor fit.

My figure dress was solid green and only had one simple detail of hot-pink piping. I wanted to jazz it up so it would fit in with the dresses of the other girls. Adding gloves to this dress was the most I could afford. I found a set of chartreuse-striped gloves. I loved them — I really believed they were snazzy — but they must have been truly hideous. Vera Wang, the skater who would grow up to become the internationally famous designer, made it to Nationals with me. She was a pairs skater with a young man named Jimmy Stewart. She commented on how well the new gloves went with my dress. Her comment bolstered me, since she was the epitome of grace and class around our rink, always wearing the most elegantly cut skating outfits, which she designed herself. Little did any of us know that her skating dresses would hold the promise of her brilliant designing career to come.

My mom, dad, and sister flew out to be with me. I did my figures with my snazzy gloves on and came in sixth place. For me, that was a huge improvement. A skater by the name of Sherry Thrappe won the figures. I was the only skater new on the national scene and we were all happy for one another. I became pals with my competitor, a quiet girl from Santa Rosa, California, named Julie McKinstry. She was the favorite to win.

Being at Nationals was so thrilling for me. I was now in the company of the best skaters not only in the country but, in some cases, the world. I soaked up as much as I could of the experience and learned as much as I could from other skaters. I was in heaven: It really was the closest thing to paradise for me. I had entered a very special club. I felt so upbeat and positive that it should have been smooth sailing for me when it was my turn to free skate. Instead, as they announced my name, I was struck with an uncontrollable panic attack, much like what I felt in school when called upon to give an answer to a question. I had never felt that panic while skating or competing before! School, yes, but not my skating! My heart began racing and I couldn't breathe. It suddenly hit me, the magnitude of being there, in the same atmosphere as my idols, like Janet Lynn. I felt trapped — I wanted to turn, run away, and never come back.

"I can't do it. I want to quit skating," I said

to Peter and Sonya, as people were cheering for me to take the ice, and I wasn't budging from my spot at the boards.

Sonya and Peter must have panicked themselves for a moment. But instead, Peter responded wisely, "Okay, you can quit skating. But go out and do this one thing first." He gave me a little push and out I went . . .

Miraculously, I skated one of my career's best performances and I won. I moved up from sixth place into first place, unheard of at the time because figures counted for 60 percent of the total score. Everyone was flabbergasted, except my mom, who seemed to expect it. When I went up to the podium, I stood on its top tier. I didn't feel I deserved the top tier because of being so inexperienced. But it did give me a boost of confidence! I was twelve and now a national champion. Julie McKinstry came in second and, thankfully, remained my friend.

My life changed immediately. I was invited to skate in dozens of local club shows on the East Coast. The invitations were a privilege and we didn't turn down one, because learning to perform was invaluable. Mom and Dad had to pay all of the travel expenses, so it got tense from time to time! Nowadays, a novice national champion can expect to earn upward of three thousand dollars for a major club show. The rules have changed. Today, the skater only has to show that the funds go toward the expenses of training and competition, which is not difficult because it all does. My generation of skaters was one of the last of Olympians skating under the old regulatory system. We had to be amateurs. Skaters were forbidden to accept any remuneration for appearances, shows, or exhibitions — or they would be considered professional. Life would certainly have been different in my home if I could have helped to pay for my skating. Perhaps that would have kept my parents from arguing, as it all would have been less stressful.

There was one exhibition I would have paid to skate in. I was invited to skate at the brand-new Madison Square Garden in a show with World and Olympic champion skaters. I was asked to be the opening number in the show. As I've mentioned, I was obsessed with the movie *The Sound of Music* and still had the edelweiss flower Mr. Lussi had given me. I loved the music from the movie and choreographed my own program to "Edelweiss" on my living room floor.

Being the reigning national Novice Ladies figure skating champion and appearing at Madison Square Garden meant nothing to my school. I was now in seventh grade.

There was no acknowledgment and I wasn't expecting it either. Instead, I was expected to take my homework with me to Seattle and reprimanded when I had not finished it upon my return. I had won a national athletic competition, trained seven hours a day, and was still expected to take gym class. I received Ds on my report card after my absence.

I didn't care that my school had no understanding of what I was doing. I loved that what I did outside of school was a secret to them. I knew that I felt at home on the ice and that it was my own special world. I didn't want school people to know about the "Skating Dorothy" because my self-confidence was so low while at school. My panic disorder never abated in class. I would rather have died than speak in front of others. I never shared these thoughts with my parents, but it was obvious to them that a public school education was not going to bend to the demands of my schedule. Thankfully, they began researching the possibility of putting me in a small tutoring school called the Yoder School in New York City. But sending me there was another matter. Jealous behavior began to erupt at the Skating Club of New York, an echo of what I had witnessed Gary Visconti suffer in Lake

Placid when his blades had been purposely damaged.

I always opened my program with a delayed Axel, my favorite jump. It served the purpose of getting my nerves under control and giving me a quick burst of energy. Once I landed it, I felt like I had gotten all the cobwebs out and was ready to perform. Girls I thought were my friends began to purposely prevent me from practicing my delayed Axel. When they heard my program music being played, they would skate over to the area where I always did it and just stand there. Many times, I could not do the jump. Peter Dunfield told me to go ahead and jump into them. My mother took great offense when she heard this and stated that I was to remain a lady no matter what.

One Saturday morning, at the usual crack of dawn, my father took me into New York for practice. The lock was broken on my locker. I opened it and my skates were gone. Sweaters, gloves, and music were all still there, but not my skates. My father immediately called the president of the club. Everyone went searching and they appeared in an unused locker in a different part of the club. No one ever found out who took them.

I didn't return to Lake Placid and to Gus Lussi that summer. The Dunfields had proven themselves invaluable to my success and didn't want their National Champion training elsewhere. They took me with them to Toronto to train at the famous Toronto Cricket, Skating and Curling Club, a luxuriously carpeted members-only club with two rinks, tennis courts, squash courts, swimming pool, cricket fields, and a fitness center. Skating of all kinds was taken very seriously in Canada, and their beautiful clubs reflected their dedication to and respect for the sport. Peter Dunfield was Canadian and he and Sonya felt very comfortable in Toronto. They rented a big home and housed several skaters there. I shared the basement with another skater. Sonya's mother cooked for the whole gang. The top Canadian skaters trained there: Ronnie Shaver, Lynn Nightingale, Toller Cranston, and Petra Burka. The Dunfields' home was the gathering spot for the skaters, and I loved babysitting their children. Little Gregory was just an infant and I realized how much I loved babies. As the baby in my family, I had had no experience with younger children, and it was a thrill for me to feel adult responsibility. It was a summer of growth in many ways. I was away from the drinking and arguing of my parents and I felt free. It showed in my skating.

Canada was more forward-thinking about the artistic side of skating. They believed it was as important as the athletic side. There were regular off-ice classes in ballet and jazz. I was guided to stretch and find positions I didn't know I could do. My flexibility had not improved very much. Every other girl still had a spiral that was much better than mine. I could never get my leg high on a spiral, no matter how hard I tried and stretched. I just wasn't born with that flexibility! But I did discover that I had flexibility in my back and learned how to do a decent layback spin. Petra Burka's mom, Ellen, was a top Canadian coach, and she led an interpretive skating class. Ms. Burka would say, "Skate like a tree," and we'd laugh at one another as we tried. Another skating club in Toronto held an interpretative skating competition in which skaters from all over Ontario would compete. Interpretive skating meant that each skater would perform to music without a choreographed and rehearsed program. The piece of music would be the same for each skater, but we wouldn't hear the music until we stepped on the ice to warm up. The musical piece would be played two times during the warm-up. Then skaters would be taken to a soundproof area before they competed. When it was my turn to skate, I kept going long after the music had stopped, not realizing that it had. I was so absorbed in interpreting the music that I didn't want it to end. While I really loved what I did, the judges didn't appreciate it. By placing me at the bottom, they were telling me I was supposed to stop when the music ended. So interpretive skating wasn't my thing!

While I really worked to develop my artistic side in skating, it was also the summer to learn a double Axel. I was moving up into Junior Ladies after passing my 6th Test, and if I was going to do well, I would have to land it. I became so bruised, falling over and over, time after time, I could barely get into the car for the ride back to the house at the end of each day. Ninety percent of skating is repetition. Skaters fall hundreds of times to learn jumps. In the mid-1980s, flying harnesses were introduced to help skaters overcome the fear of, and to prevent the injuries incurred from, this necessary body-slamming into ice. But, in my day, we didn't have that advantage. The double Axel was a jump that scared me because of the pain I felt learning it. Edge jumps had always been more difficult for me to learn than toe jumps. The Salchow and loop jumps both have a backward edge entry: Neither was a comfortable jump for me, but the forward edge takeoff on an Axel jump was the worst. It terrified me.

Gus Lussi had helped me with my double Axel, but I still didn't have it. Sonya worked with me on it. It became a major head-trip for me. It eluded me all summer. I just couldn't land my first one. I had a tough time knowing where I was in the air. My mental problem with it became more and more of a negative fixation. I had to get past it. I pushed and pushed. Nearly every skater in the rink helped me. Ronnie Shaver, who had the most beautiful double Axel of our time, would help me to try, again and again. It seemed to become the goal of several skaters at the Cricket Club that summer. They were just as frustrated watching me not land it as I was. Finally, I landed one. And then another one. And another one. Landing a jump for the first time is the most exhilarating feeling. The sense of achievement is so overwhelmingly exciting. Once you do it one time, and get that feeling, all you want to do is duplicate it. When my parents arrived to visit, they were greeted not with hellos but with complete strangers eagerly telling them, "Dorothy has her double Axel!"

Gus Lussi had tried to teach me an interesting transition between my back camel spin and my back sit spin the previous summer. I kept working on it all year. I did my best to translate what Mr. Lussi had said but it was difficult, since he was unable to demonstrate it himself. So I came up with my version of what I thought he meant. Vera Wang and her partner Jimmy Stewart were training in Toronto that summer also. Jimmy would playfully tease me about my steadfast devotion to this new spin. He'd say, "Hey, Hamill, how's your camel?" And the name stuck around. Everyone started referring to it as the Hamill Camel. It remains my trademark to this day. Just as the Axel, the Salchow, and the Lutz are named after the skaters who first performed them, I have my Hamill Camel.

The Cricket Club closed down for the last week in August for an international tennis tournament. There was only one major training center for figure skating in the East that stayed open through Labor Day, and everyone converged there. It was good old Lake Placid. I had been invited to skate in the Labor Day Show, and I was so happy to arrive back in my home-away-from-home. However, it didn't feel the same as in summers past. People treated me differently. Most people were happy for my newfound success, double Axel and all, but there were a few who didn't approve of the fact that I was going to skate in the Labor Day Show when I hadn't been there all summer long. I did understand that. Complaints were made to Bob Allen, the manager of the rink and the summer school program. He fielded them expertly. To him, it didn't matter that I hadn't trained there all summer, because he felt there were two good reasons for me to be in the show: Lake Placid was my second home, and I was National Champion.

Life changed for me drastically when we got back home to Connecticut. My parents and the Dunfields felt it would be best if I stayed in New York City all week. Patrons of the Skating Club of New York opened up their hearts and their homes to me. And that's how I found myself living in a fairy tale.

Ellen Long had a passion for ice skating and a love for those who shared her passion. She was a longtime member of the SCNY. She was an extraordinarily wealthy woman and a prominent designer. The rumor was she had decorated the White House for one of the administrations, but no one knew which one. She had a luxurious Park Avenue apartment that she shared with her eighteen-year-old daughter, Sharon Lehman, who called her mother "Mummy." The Dunfields cherished their relationship to Mrs. Long. They loved the society-page lifestyle she brought with her to the rink. She had designed and decorated the state-of-the-art Skyrink and had paid for the adults' lounge herself. When she discovered I was a promising young skater who needed a place to stay in the city, she jumped at the chance to become a part of my life.

Mrs. Long could not have been more generous to me. She kept a cook on staff who eagerly rose at five each morning to cook me a scrumptious breakfast and pack me a lunch to take with me to the rink. I could bring skating friends back with me from the rink without a moment's notice, and the cook would prepare a wonderful dinner of lamb chops for us all. A maid drew my bath and a hairdresser came every day to do Sharon and Mrs. Long's hair. There was a safe as tall as I was to hold her exquisite jewelry collection. The artwork on the walls were museum pieces. Every detail in the home was of the highest quality. The doorknob on my room was an antique pocket watch. I was in awe of the extravagance and understated elegance surrounding me. I was the country bumpkin next to the impeccably poised, elegant, well-mannered Mrs. Long and her daughter, though they never made me feel that way. They made me feel like Cinderella and I loved staying there!

There was a doorman to help me get an early morning taxi to the newly finished Skyrink. I'd take the elevator up to the sixteenth floor to a rink I instantly loved. Like the Cricket Club, the Skyrink was built only for figure skaters and had no boards surrounding it. Without any barriers, there was a greater feeling of freedom on the ice. There was no echo and no feeling of being cooped up. It had huge windows all around the ice that overlooked the New York skyline. The daylight would seep into the rink and reflect off the mirrors at one end: It was almost a holy experience as the sunrise would fill the rink each day. The only problem for my mother was its location. Skyrink was not in the best neighborhood. I hailed cabs all over New York, but the only time my mom worried about me was getting up and down that elevator every day because no one would ever know who was getting on or off. Still, I felt safe getting around and learned to be aware of my surroundings at all times. Sometimes I felt fear when I walked past construction sites and workers called out to me or whistled. At the time, I mostly took it in stride, but as I look back now, I should have warned the adults in my life.

I'd skate until noon. Then I'd hail another cab to the Yoder School. There were only twelve of us in our class and we all had special circumstances that prevented us from attending regular school. One girl was a beautiful model, one boy could not stop rocking and twitching, another was a belligerent, tough-talking rebel. It was a small schoolhouse in the middle of the biggest urban center in the world, yet we were all given individual attention. I'd only have to put in a few hours in class and then I'd get myself back to the Skyrink. I eventually learned the bus system and started taking the bus to save my precious dollars. Despite the fear of the construction sites, I sometimes walked to save on bus fare. I didn't tell anyone I was doing this. When I had saved twenty dollars, I went to Alexander's and bought myself an outfit. When my mom saw this outfit, I lied, making up a story that Mrs. Long's daughter, Sharon, had given it to me, because I didn't want to tell her I was walking everywhere. Sometimes I'd play hooky from school and stay at the rink to skate. Occasionally, I'd get caught by my mom, who would track my whereabouts through spies at the rink or my teacher at the Yoder School. Even though Mom was an hour's drive away, it didn't seem I could get away with much. The leash was still there, which was good, and it was short, which made it better, but I still actually thought I was okay on my own.

When Mrs. Long died, in the late 1970s, my mother and I went to her funeral. The church was packed and we had to stand way in the back. I had difficulty hearing the speakers. When her son rose to speak about his mother, he began to tell the story of a little girl she had helped to achieve her dream. It was only when he said "Olympic champion" that I realized he was talking about me. Mrs. Long would never take a dime from my parents. She and another SCNY family, the Streeters, made it possible for me to live in the most incredible city in the world so I could continue my training. I can never thank these people enough.

I went to Nationals in 1970, very prepared in Junior Ladies. I was ready to perform my double Axel and Hamill Camel for the first time in competition. To get my mind off the pressure, my parents continued the tradition they had started in Intermediate Ladies. They found a miniature golf course nearby. It was always an easy and fun distraction and it certainly worked here. I won the silver medal. In first place was my good friend and pen pal, Julie McKinstry. Afterward, we stayed up all night, talking and laughing.

Back at my home club, relationships with skaters who were competitive with me weren't so rosy. Tensions began to mount over my parents' decision to move me up into Senior Ladies for the following year. The Dunfields thought I was too young for Senior Ladies and wanted me to stay in Juniors for one more year so that I had a chance of winning it. But my parents knew there were many more opportunities in Senior Ladies for a skater. The top ten were invited into international competitions and gained invaluable experience at venues worldwide, as international judges came to know them. My mother believed that the Dunfields had another motive for holding me back. They announced that they were going to coach another competitor, and she was in the Senior Ladies division. This skater was a bit older than I and more experienced but, most important, had a wealthy benefactor who could pay for far more lessons than my parents could afford. The wealthy family and the Dunfields were convinced that this skater had a better chance at the following year's Nationals than I did. I began to get less and less attention from the Dunfields.

In order to move into Senior Ladies, the Gold, or 8th, figure test must be passed. The twelve different sets of figures on this test, the highest level to be achieved, were by far the most complicated and intricate, more difficult than all the other tests combined. It took a minimum of one year, perhaps two years, of intense concentration on these figures in order to pass them. This was why it was impossible to have a fourteen- or fifteen-year-old win a world or Olympic championship. Since no one could believe I was strong enough in figures yet, the idea of moving up seemed like a pipe dream.

Even though I was not their number-one pupil, I went to Toronto with the Dunfields for the summer again. The previous summer had been so rewarding, and I held steadfast to those positive memories. I focused on my Gold Test and managed to pass it in Canada. I felt it would serve as a good warm-up to taking it in the United States, but the Dunfields weren't all that impressed. They felt that U.S. standards were tougher. The Dunfields procrastinated on my program choreography, and my parents had to drive up to Toronto to push them to finish editing my music. It came down to the last minute as my dad stayed up all night getting the tapes done with Peter Dunfield, then raced back, driving to D.C. for a 7 A.M. meeting.

In the fall, I passed my U.S. Gold figure

Test, the 8th and final figure test. I became eligible for Senior Ladies. I was fourteen years old.

Ritter Shumway was the president of the USFSA at that time. An interesting report came to my parents from an ice dancer who had paired up with him at a recent dance weekend. This woman pulled my mother aside at the Skating Club one day. She quoted Mr. Shumway, "If the Hamills were smart, they would get Dorothy out of New York. The Dunfields will keep her behind the older girls." By "older girls" he meant those maybe two years older than I. But in skating, two years meant a lot more experience.

My mother's instincts about my situation had been verified.

But it was right before my first senior Nationals. I couldn't abruptly change coaches now. We went to Buffalo in the middle of a winter blizzard with fifty-five-mile-per-hour winds; we had to hold on to light posts to stand up. The stormy weather paralleled the storm brewing inside the arena. I skated well and came in fifth. Janet Lynn, the skater I most admired and attempted to emulate, won. I was honored to be in the same competition with her. Julie Lynn Holmes won silver; Suna Murray, another great skater, won bronze; and Dawn Glab was fourth. To this day, I cannot remember the placement of the skater who had the wealthy backing except to say I was ahead of her. After this, we thought for sure I would get the attention I needed from the Dunfields, but I'm truly sorry to admit that this lovely couple who did so much for me were never given the chance to redeem themselves. The Olympic Committee of the USFSA intervened. They invited Julie Lynn Holmes and me to represent the United States in an event that the Japanese were hosting in anticipation of the following year's Olympics.

It was called the Pre-Olympics and was a trial run for the Japanese to practice their international hosting skills. I was invited because both Janet Lynn and Suna Murray were going to the North Americans, a competition between the United States and Canada held during the same week. Julie Lynn Holmes decided against competing in the North Americans because she felt she had little chance of winning and wanted to get international exposure for the following year's Olympics. My parents and I knew it was the next big leap in my skating career. It was my international debut. Carl Gram, an important judge on the Olympic Committee, told my parents that I would be accompanied by Carlo Fassi, since he coached Julie

Lynn Holmes and we could go together. My mother asked if they could send Sonya Dunfield as my coach, but they refused, insisting that they could not pay her way — yet they were willing to pay my mother's way as a chaperone. It seemed the Olympic Committee was doing its part to maneuver me toward another coach, Mr. Fassi. And we weren't about to dispute it on its choice.

Carlo was an Italian skater who had won the European championship in 1953 and 1954. He began coaching and made his mark early. After the 1961 plane crash killed our American figure skating team, the USFSA asked him to move to the United States to help rebuild figure skating in our country. He took up residence at the Broadmoor in Colorado Springs and it didn't take him long to put the Americans back on the international map. His student, Peggy Fleming, won the Olympics in 1968. I certainly knew of Carlo Fassi and his impeccable reputation as a brilliant coach for school figures, which I really needed at this stage of my skating. Even more important, he had great respect among international judges, an asset any emerging international skater absolutely needed. Now I was on a plane with him going to Japan. I was surprised and delighted that he had such a great sense of humor. He was forty-one years old and in his prime. I immediately felt comfortable with him.

We arrived in Tokyo and boarded buses bound for Sapporo. It took hours, and the buses were tiny, even for me. We laughed the whole way. Carlo was so much fun to be with, our sides ached from laughing at all the stories he shared with us. We arrived at our Sapporo hotel after our twenty-hour travel day only to be told they did not have rooms for us. Carlo made a scene, knowing the hospitable Japanese would be horrified, declaring, "Then we go home!" Suddenly, Julie Lynn and I had a room. We were paired with two skiers who would arrive back at the hotel in the middle of the night after their long ride back from the mountain each day. Julie and I had to get up early each morning for our practices. It was an illogical room match, but at least we had a room while the Japanese worked out the kinks. The Japanese knew little about figure skating at that time. But they were anxious to learn and began to produce international champions by the 1990s, like the incredible Midori Ito, who was the first woman to land a triple Axel in competition, and Yuka Sato, so powerful and delicate at the same time, who won the 1994 Worlds. Our experience taught us that the Japanese people were the kindest and most welcoming people we had ever met. The competition ran like clockwork. They did a masterful job running the Pre-Olympics and had nothing to worry about for the 1972 Olympic Games.

Sometime during this trip, my mother and I looked at each other and had the same thought. Despite our acrimonious relationship and also perhaps because of it, we could each feel what the other was thinking. We knew the next move. It would be to Carlo Fassi.

4
Go West, Young Skater

Our move wouldn't take us to the beautiful Broadmoor in Colorado Springs. We were told Carlo Fassi had had a falling out there, so a rink was being built for him in Denver by a group of investors. It would have two sheets of ice, and Fassi would be able to run it the way he wanted. While it was under construction, he needed a place to go with his skaters — hard-working competitors like Ronnie Shaver and Lynn Nightingale, who sought more international exposure and got it with Fassi. Julie Lynn Holmes was from Tulsa, Oklahoma, and its skating club took us in with open arms. They rented two side-by-side condos for Fassi's older skaters, who could live on their own. The younger skaters were allowed to hang out there, but lived elsewhere with a chaperone. Fassi and his wife, Crista, offered to take me in for the summer until my mother could move there and put together an apartment for us. Tulsa was a culture shock for a young girl who had become accustomed to navigating big city life. The heat was unbearable — thank heaven we were in an ice rink all day long — but the people were nice in a way I hadn't known and I loved it.

Staying at the Fassis' was also a form of culture shock and not just because Crista was sixteen years younger than Carlo. She was a German skater who had traveled to Italy to train with him. Not long after, they had fallen in love. It must have been a scandal at the time in Europe, but here in America, no one ever spoke of it because there was no reason to. He was a typically old-fashioned European man when it came to his family life. He was a good provider, a loving husband and father, and he treasured his time with his family. While he was demanding at the rink, to the point of intimidating parents, skaters, and other coaches, he knew how to turn it off when he came home. Crista was a beautiful and elegant woman. She coached the intermediate skaters, but put Carlo's career first because she understood his passion for the sport and the dedication it took to train an Olympic champion. She worshipped him and helped him to be successful.

Crista loved being a mom and homemaker, and every night there was a family dinner in their house. They had two young children at the time. Everyone was expected to pitch in and help, including me. Life at the Fassis' gave me a first glimpse into how normal happy families behave. There was a kindness and respect for family members I hadn't experienced before. There was never any yelling and nobody ever seemed at odds. They made a happy life together. I didn't feel homesick for my own family because our home life had never been quite like this. It was wonderful to be in an apartment with a family so full of life.

Then Mom came out to set up our own apartment, and sent me to summer school to take two courses at Holland Hall, a small private school in Tulsa.

Carlo asked her, "Why do you bother with school in the summer?"

"She must catch up on schoolwork she missed by going to Japan."

Carlo was more pointed. Half seriously, half joking he asked, "Why do you bother with school at all? She will make lots of money coaching."

My mother was indignant. "I want her to be educated, just in case." She lost her sense of humor when talking to Carlo.

"In case of what?"

"In case of injury. In case none of this works out, she has to have an education. It's a priority."

Clearly, Carlo did not make it a priority. My mother and Carlo were not starting off on the best of terms. She immediately felt an added stress of responsibility because she did not have support for my education from the person designated by the USFSA as my new coach. It's hard for me to know if Carlo was really serious about not bothering with school. I guess he believed my love of skating was so powerful it would always take care of me.

Fortunately, one of those courses panned out for me immediately. It was my French class. I was invited to compete in the back-to-back competitions at Saint-Gervais, France, and Obertsdorf, West Germany. It was important for me to be seen by the international judges. It was also crucial to get to know the East German skaters who weren't allowed to compete at Saint-Gervais and Obertsdorf. They dominated international Senior Ladies. There was an East German coach, Frau Mueller, who taught all the top skaters, Gabriele Seyfert, Sonja Morgenstern, and Annette Poetsch. She also had the up-and-coming Katarina Witt. If I had any hope of competing at their level, I had to know what they were doing, what music they were using, what they were wearing, and what new moves they had mastered. Competition was not the time to study other skaters. In fact, I had to insulate myself at competition time. I tried to find areas within the arena where I could not hear the applause for the previous skater. Cheering for hard-won jumps or gasping over a fall would distract me from keeping my own program in my head. So I understood that being invited to Saint-Gervais was very important for me. It would give me the time to watch my competitors without my own performance being jeopardized.

Back in Tulsa, my mom and I were invited to a Fourth of July picnic at the home of Dr. Hugh C. Graham and his wife, Beth. They were both judges and had two young daughters who skated. The Grahams would become two of my most trusted advisors as I climbed up the ladder of international competition.

Our lovely setup with the Skating Club of Tulsa was to last only one summer. The construction on the Denver rink was behind schedule and Carlo needed to take his skaters elsewhere. There was one place we could always count on.

It was Lake Placid. Off we went to spend

the whole winter there. Mom enrolled me in Lake Placid High School. I was fourteen, just like all the other ninth graders, some of whom I already knew from my earlier years spent in the town. While my mom felt she had my educational needs well taken care of, our living needs were another matter. The garage apartment we had been able to rent inexpensively for two summers on Humdinger Hill was not winterized. We always had to look for ways to save, so of course, we found ways to save on rent. The cheapest Mom could find was a one-room efficiency in a house owned by former show skaters. It was on the south side of town, across the street from the only grocery store. The room was so small that the door couldn't open completely. The bathroom we shared with other guests was down the hall. It constantly smelled of gas from the leaking oven. The best thing I can say about this place was that it was always toasty and warm. The room was a far cry from my fairy-tale existence in Ellen Long's Fifth Avenue apartment, but it was home, temporarily. We never questioned that we would do anything differently. You do what is necessary to follow the coach who taught Olympic Champion Peggy Fleming. Here, in this tiny, gassy room, I began to think that maybe I could make it to the

Olympic team. It didn't seem so far-fetched anymore. Somehow, my mom made Thanksgiving dinner in this tiny room. She cooked a turkey in the leaky oven and invited Carlo, Julie Lynn, Julie Lynn's mother, and Ronnie Shaver. My dad drove up and we sat crunched together in this room where the door could not fully open. I'm not sure how we all fit in there at the same time. I guessed if my mom could pull together that fun dinner under those challenging conditions, complete with laughs, and a tasty turkey besides, then maybe I had a shot at the Olympics.

To me, it was always a given that I owed my family something for all their self-sacrifice. It wasn't only my parents. I felt I owed my brother and sister. They certainly did their part to help. I didn't complain, nor did my mom, about our paltry surroundings in Lake Placid when I knew Marcia and Sandy were working to earn their own way. Marcia changed bedpans at a nursing home while Sandy worked so diligently at Exeter that he won the Tad Jones scholarship to study pre-med at Yale, covering much of his tuition, and worked setting up labs to buy his books. My skate boots cost ninety-five dollars and the blades cost over a hundred. I always needed two pairs at a time, figure and free skate, and went through a pair of each every year, totaling almost four hundred dollars. Four hundred bucks would have bought a lot of books. Skates or books — my parents had to agonize over every dollar.

I was so embedded in my quest that it felt like we were all on a snowball and it was gaining speed and size, and there was no getting off. Even when I became very ill that winter, I was not about to get off the snowball. Shortly before the 1972 Long Beach Nationals, I came down with the flu and it would not go away. Weak with a high fever and glassy-eyed, I insisted that I keep skating. My mother took me to the trusted Dr. Hart, the doctor who had pierced my ears just three years before. He could feel my determination. He told my mom that if she bundled me up, I could keep training for Nationals. Bless his heart for trying. My mother wouldn't listen and she took me back to our rooming house and put me straight to bed. I stayed there for a week. It didn't make a difference and I arrived in Long Beach still very ill, but the California sunshine brightened my spirits.

During this illness I lost almost ten pounds, which made me physically very weak. My mom watched over me like a hawk. After I put on my skates, she'd get me out of the dressing room so that I wouldn't hear the talk of the other skaters. She'd take me into the bathroom. There we'd find Janet Lynn, doing the same thing with her coach, Slavka Kahout. All things considered, I skated well, which surprised me as well as everyone who knew how sick I was. So when I came in fourth, just missing a berth on the 1972 Olympic team, I was crushed and disappointed. One judge had me in thirteenth place because she didn't like my footwork. That was a new one for me. I didn't know my footwork was so hopeless. Of course I was hurt by the judge's comment, but I was in a subjective sport and that came with the territory. I was happy I had skated as well as I had, so the defeat wasn't devastating when it happened. It was a couple weeks later, when I got my strength back, that it hit me. Another judge had said to my mother, "I wish I had known Dorothy had been so sick," implying he would have placed me third if he had known I could not possibly be skating my best. I knew my mom was angry. If I had been good enough — then it would have been different.

Meanwhile, I had been receiving fan mail from Japan for almost a whole year. The Japanese had gotten to know me the previous year at the Pre-Olympics and had expected to see me back for the Olympics. I didn't realize I had made such an impact over there until officials told me the Japanese had kept my name up in the dressing room the entire year. I felt a great sense of loss at not making the team. There was an overwhelming emotion echoing inside of me that my destiny might not be what I wanted.

Meanwhile, Carlo sensed something none of us could have considered. He advised my parents, "Take her back to Lake Placid and keep her training." I didn't know why he told them this, especially when I really needed a break from training. But my dutiful mom and I went back to Lake Placid and I tried to keep up my same training schedule. I heard news about the Olympics the way all Americans did, a day later. I remember watching the lovely Janet Lynn skate. Beatrice "Trixie" Schuba won the gold, Karen Magnusson of Canada won the silver, and Janet Lynn the bronze. Julie Lynn Holmes did not place. She was the sweetest, loveliest champion I had ever met. What a role model I had in her, and I was so fortunate to practice with her.

By this time, I had almost gotten over the heartbreak that I had been so close to making the Olympic team. I knew I had to wait my turn like everybody else. Then, two days after the Olympics, Mom got a phone call from the USFSA. They asked me to compete in the world championships, which are always held a couple of weeks after the Olympics. Julie Lynn Holmes had assumed she was not going to win a medal in Worlds, given that she hadn't at the Olympics. So she had chosen to turn professional and signed a contract with an ice show. I was selected to take her place on the World Team. I'd never dreamed I'd be invited to Worlds that year, but maybe Carlo had known all along. Although I had competed internationally in Sapporo and Saint-Gervais, Worlds was different, because every top skater from each country would be there. I was overjoyed, but my mom took this opportunity to slam the judges. Her anger from Nationals had not abated and she pulled no punches when she spouted, "They could have placed you third. You should have gone to the Olympics." Well, I knew I hadn't deserved to be there, and in the end it had worked out well! But ever the negative mom, she couldn't find joy over the decision to send me to Worlds: Instead, she seemed to dwell on the fact her child had been slighted. I took this to mean that fourth place in the country wasn't good enough for her, the judges' opinions weren't good enough for her, and I wasn't up to her standards. I was only fourteen: I couldn't possibly have had the perspective I have today of her actions and attitude. It has taken me many years of soul-searching to try to understand her perspective. It was simple: Like most moms, she wanted the world to know that her daughter deserved the best and was the most talented. She wanted to protect her child from disappointment. What she didn't realize was that although it was tough to miss it by one placement, I wasn't disappointed. She was.

Worlds held in Calgary, Alberta, Canada. Fortunately, my dad was able to attend the competition. He could take the heat off Mom. Somehow, they made it seem as if we were on a vacation and put no pressure on me between practices. We drove up to gaze at Lake Louise and then ate at the landmark Banff Springs Hotel. I skated quite well and placed fifth, much higher than anyone expected. It probably made my mother feel vindicated about her instincts that I should have been on the Olympic team. I was the fifth-best skater in the world. Wow! I have to admit, that was a real boost to my confidence. I had officially arrived on the international figure-skating scene. Now, if I could only pass ninth-grade English!

I went back to Lake Placid High to finish

the school year, happy to be with my friends. It would have been nice to spend the summer there, but the Denver Ice Arena was ready. The Fassi brigade of students migrated there. This mountain city would be my home base for the next four years. I hadn't had the comfort of living in one place since I'd started skating: I'd felt like a gypsy since I was nine. I thought I would have comfort here in Denver, staying in one place. Not so. My mom and I kept moving around to keep the shorter, less expensive apartment leases. When she couldn't stay with me, I'd live with another skater's family.

It wasn't long after settling into Denver that I was on the road again. I was invited to skate in a summer tour overseas, in Europe and behind the Iron Curtain. Carlo thought it would be a great experience for me. Of course I loved the opportunity! To skate with the East German skaters behind the Iron Curtain meant going into a mysterious world, but thankfully, Carlo knew how to play the international game and I was now one of his students. The East Germans were our greatest rivals, but he was unafraid of them, unlike so many in the United States. At competitions he would walk right up to their judges and referees to ask, "What's the talk?" "What's in now?" "What are you looking for?" He taught me I must be open with them and show them who I was.

First, Mom and I flew to meet the other skaters in West Germany, then Switzerland, then to East Germany. I was shocked! Everything there was gray and colorless, from the people's faces to the buildings. Even the sky seemed gray, as if the sun had suddenly stopped shining. The Berlin Wall had armed guards pacing back and forth. We all felt the lack of freedom and were scared to do anything wrong. I was now considered a world-class competitor and I was expected to represent my country in a manner befitting our great nation. We were not allowed to be paid for our performances but the International Skating Union (ISU) allotted us five dollars a day for food. When we were in East Germany, we were given their currency, marks, but there was nothing to buy. We weren't able to exchange them for Western currency when we crossed back over to the West. So we all pooled our marks and handed them to a young male East German skater we had met. We knew he could use the money for his needs. As we were taking off from the train station, we handed the wad to him out the train window. We thought we were doing him a gigantic favor, but as he took the money, there was only terror in his eyes. He was a promising skater and we never heard from him again. I have discussed this with my fellow tour-mates since then and we only hope that our gesture of goodwill didn't get him banned from international skating for life!

Living and touring with skaters from behind the Iron Curtain opened my eyes to the way others lived, in a way I never could have imagined. I knew their skaters were extremely well trained. But they were starved for basic human needs. For instance, the venues we skated in would always have fruit baskets waiting for us in the locker rooms. The East bloc skaters would rush in ahead of us and grab the fruit as if they hadn't seen oranges and apples before. Bananas were their favorite, the rarest fruit of all for them. We learned to purposely not eat the fruit and leave it all for them because it was so precious to them. They acted so secretive about taking it, as if they were stealing something and were afraid of getting caught. I was just turning fifteen and was wide-eyed at their behavior. It was explained to me that these skaters or their parents would stand in line for hours to get such treats in their country. We have such abundance in this country — it was hard to imagine waiting in line for one or two oranges.

The East bloc skaters were our toughest

competition, because they were essentially professional skaters. Their government subsidized their training, living, travel, and competition expenses. They had the job of working on their skating full-time. Their parents didn't have to deal with the financial pressure of raising a skater, the way Western parents did. We felt amateurish in their presence, and we were, by comparison. But we also knew that these skaters had other stresses we did not, emotional strains we could not relate to. They had to give up a part of themselves to be controlled by their government. They were removed from their homes and had to live far away from their families. Their parents were never allowed to travel with them to competitions. It was a privilege for one's child to be taken to a national training center. It was what every parent wanted for their children. But the government felt the skater would defect if their parents were with them at competitions. By keeping the parents at home, there was some guarantee the skater would return. The best the parents could do to see their children skate was to watch them on TV.

When I arrived back home after these trips, I was more grateful than ever for the freedom afforded us by our system. Although dollars thrown our way would have eased my family's crisis, I knew in those days I could not have it both ways. I was always proud to represent my country, but I did not want to skate for a government. For decades, the East bloc skaters represented a cold and intimidating presence at international competitions. But that has changed with the tearing down of the Berlin Wall and the break-up of the USSR into states. While the skaters continue to get healthy subsidies from their countries, now they are seen as people first, not their government's machines. Interestingly, it is China that has adapted the old system. Children are selected at a very young age and molded to become champions. Oftentimes, they have to move thousands of miles away from home, away from their parents, living apart from them for years. And they currently dominate the world of figure skating.

The following year I returned to East Germany with my brother, Sandy, who accompanied me in place of my mom. Sandy spoke German fluently and loved all things German. It was a great opportunity for us to spend time together: Between his education and my skating, we had rarely seen each other. The way I adored my brother had not abated, so I cherished any time I had with him. The trip evoked wonderful memories from my pre-skating days, when our parents had taken us on road trips along the East Coast. They'd combined my father's business trips to Washington, D.C., with stops at the Lincoln Memorial, the Washington Monument, and, my favorite of all, Monticello. I also remembered one trip when they'd taken us to the Luray Caverns in Virginia, one of the world's most spectacular natural wonders, because Sandy was fascinated by geology. Those trips were made on a dime, my parents making peanut-butter sandwiches along the way and staying at the cheapest place they could find. Sometimes we even slept in sleeping bags in the car. So now this was an opportunity of a lifetime for us to go to Europe together, as representatives of our country.

Sandy was happy to be with me and to be able to use his second language. The East German officials, however, did *not* like him speaking German to their skaters. They became suspicious of Sandy. Who knows, maybe they thought he was going to help them escape to America. Yeah, right! They watched his every move. He joked facetiously that the lamps in the hotel rooms were bugged and talked into the lampshades as if people were listening to us: I thought he had read too many spy novels. But when we came back through Checkpoint Charlie, all of his books were confiscated, even his copy of *The Old Man and the Sea*. He couldn't understand why Hemingway would offend them, but he wasn't about to argue. He realized that these people took their government jobs seriously. When we returned to the good old U.S. of A., there was a letter from the USFSA stating as kindly as possible that Sandy would not be invited back to tour with me. Oh, well, everyone loved him and his outrageous sense of humor. We still laugh about that trip.

Beginning sophomore year of high school at Kennedy High in Denver turned out to be a disaster. By state law, they couldn't be lenient about my scheduling conflicts. If I missed six days of school, I would have to repeat the courses. So, between competitions and practice and travel, you can see the train wreck coming! Traveling back and forth to Toronto to get my music and choreography done by Ellen Burka, I was a gypsy again that school year and couldn't adhere to Colorado state law. Carlo was too busy teaching figures and free skating to choreograph programs. Besides, he admittedly didn't like doing it and wasn't very good at it. That skating season, in 1973, introduced the short program to competition, which meant doubling up on practice time in free skating. Ellen Burka picked out two pieces of music for my short program and I was to choose the one I liked best. One was a very complex violin piece, which, she said, "would be difficult to skate to but would stand out." She was very protective of this piece: She wouldn't tell me the title of it because she feared others might use it. Naturally, I chose this piece and I still don't know the name of it or its composer.

Next, I was off to England for the Richmond Hill competition in London, and then to Prague, Czechoslovakia, for another competition. The USFSA paid for one chaperone and Dad came with me. Carlo urged me to visit Bratislava, Czechoslovakia, after the competition in Prague to check out the arena where Worlds would be held the following year. I stood in the old, cold arena, envisioning myself here in just five months. It was a whirlwind trip and this was just the first semester of school. There was no way I was going to be able to meet Colorado state law requirements for my schooling.

Nationals were held in Minneapolis that year. I came in second to Janet Lynn. It was a milestone for me. Janet Lynn had been my favorite skater and my inspiration since I first had seen her skate in Lake Placid when

I was ten years old. Now, just five years later, I had won the short program and had beaten her. It was the first year of the short program, and it was to my advantage because now my weakness, figures, counted for only 40 percent of the total score whereas before it had been 60 percent. I have Janet Lynn to thank for that monumental change in skating: It occurred after the world was shocked, watching her lose the Olympics to Trixie Schuba after the free skate. Janet was the best free skater in the world and Trixie had the best figures in the world, but the audience did not realize figures had set the placements, before Janet had even gotten on the ice.

Before the U.S. team went to Bratislava, we trained in Innsbruck for two weeks. The USFSA put us in a small *pensione* with no restaurant nearby. We had to walk miles into a village to get something to eat. It was freezing cold, and snowy. And we had no car. Janet Lynn struggled with asthma her entire skating career, but these walks crippled her and she could not make them. We would bring her food. She didn't feel well during the whole competition in Bratislava. She turned professional immediately after and joined the Ice Follies. I placed fourth. I was thrilled. I knew my turn to win a medal would come.

Back at the Denver rink, there were plenty of other skaters who shared my dilemma of trying to fit school into our schedules. Many of them gave up on traditional schooling and resorted to homeschooling and tutors. My mom was insistent that I stay in a school atmosphere to keep my life as normal as possible. Joe DeLio was a skating father who worked at Kennedy High and also became known for being one of the greatest skate-sharpeners in the world. He managed to help me get credit for one of my classes and to set up my summer school. But I couldn't do summer school either because I was expected to tour in Europe. So I did a summer correspondence course for another class. Mom finally gave up on the public school system and visited a small private school, Colorado Academy. We knew about this school because its hockey team practiced and played games at the Denver Ice Arena. It would add to the cost of my skating, but somehow we had to figure out a way to make it happen. Mom took me to the headmaster of the school and told him what we were up against. He was completely sympathetic and said the school could work around the demands of a world competitive skater. We felt happy to have found a solution to my educational problems and requirements, and I was very excited to start over in a lovely small school and meet some new friends outside of skating. Things seemed to be running smoothly. But in skating, things — besides the ice — were never smooth. Case in point — I was then invited to perform in the Cleveland Ice Show.

The Cleveland Ice Show is an annual event that draws top U.S. skaters, and as the runner-up to our national champion, I was expected to be there. But the training for Worlds, and the fourteen-city European exhibition tour that followed, caused tendonitis in my Achilles and I needed rest. The searing pain was unbearable! Just as importantly, I had promised the headmaster of Colorado Academy that I would be attending school as soon as I returned from Europe. Mom and Dad informed the Cleveland Skating Club that I would not be able to perform in their event, which was a marathon of five shows, three evening and two matinees, over a weekend. I wanted to do it but we were sorry: With such short notice it wouldn't be possible this year. We thought that would be the end of the story. It wasn't.

Soon, my parents received a telegram from a USFSA judge, a member of the Cleveland

Club. Together with his wife, they comprised one of the most powerful judging teams in the United States. The telegram essentially said that it was my duty to skate in the Cleveland show, and if I didn't, they would find a more suitable champion next year. My parents were outraged! My mother took this as a threat. If I wasn't going to cooperate, these judges might find retribution by marking me down in the next competition. It was, after all, one of these judges who had marked me thirteenth two years prior when she didn't like my footwork, preventing me from making the Olympic team.

My mom took the telegram to the Colorado Academy headmaster and slapped it on his desk, exclaiming, "What am I supposed to do with this?" She was desperate and looking to him to help us figure out how to combine school with competitions, practices, exhibitions, and travel. This meant I wouldn't be in classes that week and my promise of finishing my schoolwork on time meant nothing. But up until that point, the headmaster hadn't fully understood the pressure we were under. Now he was so sympathetic. All of this was new to him, too. He just rolled with it and said, "Come into school on Sunday when you get back and we'll work it out." What amazes me is that my parents were paying for the private school, and my skating expenses, yet the Association was insisting I make appearances for them. I went and skated the five shows. I took the schoolbooks with me. And smiled through the excruciating pain in my tendon.

There were so many good people associated with the USFSA that this story stands out. The judges, officials, and referees were not paid by the organization. They all volunteered their time because they felt a passion for the sport, just as we skaters were required to volunteer our time for shows. Clearly, I wasn't accustomed to my new role as the potential favorite to be the next U.S. champion.

At the same time, I had another role to fill — that of a teenager. And that meant boys. I really liked boys and enjoyed hanging out with them. There was one in particular I really liked, Tom Regan. He and I had a lot in common. He was a figure skater so he understood the curfew I had. His father was one of the investors who had built the rink for Fassi. I was very limited in the amount of time I could spend with him, not only because of my training, travel, and competitive and school schedules, but also because of my mother. She didn't want me staying out late or else I'd be too tired the next day to train.

I'd finish practice by seven thirty and be allowed to get a Coke or take in a hockey game with my boyfriend.

Then there was a guy I had met in Germany who was not a skater. His name was Egbert and I was quite taken by him. We'd had a one-week romance in West Germany when I was touring there and my mom was alarmed to see him appear in Colorado. Somehow the West Germans found out about this and the West German coach called Carlo. He was told "Eggie" was ". . . from a bad family and Dorothy should not have anything to do with him." Just as fast as he was in my life, he was out of it. He certainly seemed like a nice guy to me.

While my parents and coach felt I had to be protected from German boys, my teenage years were not lived under an entirely protective cover. I did all the normal things other teenagers did. On weekends, we'd pile as many kids as possible into one car to crash a drive-in movie theater. We'd climb into the trunk and sneak in, just like kids did all over. There were weekends when I couldn't join in the fun because I'd be expected to skate in a show out of town. There were weekend trips with the Colorado Academy that I could not participate in. I remember a canoe trip I would have loved to go on and couldn't. But I did not miss my prom.

My teenage rebellions involved smoking cigarettes and drinking Kahlúa in McDonald's milkshakes. I tried smoking to control my weight and I did it without my mom knowing. Or so I thought. Once she caught me and was enraged. But her reaction wasn't as harsh as I thought it would be — maybe because she was a smoker. Fortunately, I didn't smoke for very long or very much at a time. As for the drinking, I experimented a little, like the other teenagers. Kahlúa was the popular drink among our crowd. I didn't like the taste of alcohol, so we would buy McDonald's milkshakes and pour the Kahlúa into it. But Kahlúa was expensive and a bottle of it could get consumed quickly, not to mention the calories — yikes! So a friend of mine, a fellow skater, started making her own homemade brand of "Kahlúa" from vodka. Rebellion and experimentation are hallmarks of teenagers as we begin to separate from our parents. But I couldn't completely separate. I was financially dependent on my parents so I could keep skating. Here, for the four years we were to be in Colorado, I was especially dependent on my mother. We were glued together, for better and for worse.

The various apartments my mom rented

while we were in Denver were sometimes within walking distance of the rink, so that we could save on gas. The rink was in an industrial part of town, so it wasn't the most pleasant section to live in. I could feel my mom's resentment growing, having to live away from home and struggle to make ends meet. She glared and snarled at me at the rink if she didn't think I was working hard enough. I knew I had to make it worth her while. But at the same time, I felt there wasn't anything that would make her happy.

Yet she was capable of such love and sacrifice that when I think of it now, it still breaks my heart. I recall one night around dinnertime when Mom drove me to the grocery store, gave me five dollars from her purse, and said, "Go get something to eat." My dad had not been able to send her a check that week. It wasn't until later that I realized Mom had given me her last five dollars. She had unselfishly told me to get something to eat and went hungry herself.

We didn't have extra money to do things like the other skaters, so we made the best of our situation. I decided to start baking, since flour and sugar were cheap, and were usually on hand in the apartment. I found a recipe on the side of a cereal box. It was called Granola Date Coffee Cake and I actually thought it was healthy just because it had granola in it! Its main ingredients were butter and sugar. All I knew was that it was delicious, fun to make, and I loved granola. I kept on baking fatty goods because of my insatiable craving for sugar. These are some of the happiest memories I have of living with my mother in Denver: at any other time, she was interminably critical of me, but not when I was baking.

Her criticisms were the result of her own pessimistic way of thinking. I don't know if it was the way she was raised and her own frustrations with unfinished goals. Perhaps those frustrations made her feel she was incapable of coping with the pressures of being a skating mom. I had an innate sense that I could fight off her negativity by showing her that I could be good enough. An athlete cannot perform at her best if she lacks confidence, and I constantly needed to find it anywhere I could. When I saw Julie Lynn Holmes reading *The Power of Positive Thinking* by Norman Vincent Peale, I was very curious. She said it inspired her and she let me read it. I couldn't put it down. I didn't know my mother saw me reading it until one day she presented me with a gift. It was my very own copy of the book. She must have felt there was something that she couldn't teach me.

The book became my mantra for giving me the mental strength to compete and to win. I read and reread it all through my teenage years and all the way through to the Olympics. It was one of the greatest gifts she gave me. My mother didn't know how to raise an Olympic champion — what parent does? — but she knew to buy me that book, which confused me. What she didn't realize was how much her negative attitude and lack of approval angered me.

Other people noticed my mother's downbeat, difficult manner and its effect on me. The skaters would talk behind her back and make comments. Some were actually afraid of her. She became aware of her reputation and it made her defensive. She'd walk into the rink and the kids would stop talking. Once, a boy let out an inadvertent chuckle after they had all quieted down. Assuming he was laughing at her, she snapped back, "I don't know what you're laughing at. It's not very funny!" I was mortified.

Worse, Carlo was beginning to blame my mother's demeanor for my recent changes in behavior. I had become a rebellious teenage brat, taking to kicking the ice and swearing like a sailor if I made a mistake. He told my mother that she made me nervous. Of course, it was her fault, not mine. Ha! Naturally, she began to feel resentful toward him. Carlo and I could tell what kind of mood my mother was in the second she walked into the rink. It was written all over her face. And it was rarely good for me. She felt the world was out to get me and I couldn't convince her otherwise. At competitions, officials would roll their eyes at my mother. They thought I didn't see, but I did. I wanted so much for her to lighten up, to not say anything. It was so confusing. Nothing I did was good enough for her, yet when she spoke to others, I could see she believed in me. I was wrong to want Mom not to be so outspoken, but I was too young to know that she was up against the sport's old boys' network. If my father said something to officials to protect my interests, like rescheduling a plane flight so I could get a good night's sleep, he would be respected and my wish granted. If my mother stood up to them and made a similar request, she would be treated differently, disrespected, tagged and stereotyped as an impossible woman on a tirade.

Doris Fleming, Peggy Fleming's mother, was another mother who was stigmatized by an undeserved reputation of being a witchy skating mother — all mothers who spoke out were — yet she was one of the kindest women I have ever met. Since Doris's own daughter had been coached by Carlo, she knew that he lacked choreographic skills. Mrs. Fleming offered to be my host if I wanted to fly to Los Angeles to have my choreography done by Robert Paul. Bob Paul and his partner, Barbara Wagner, had won the Gold Medal in Pairs at the 1960 Winter Olympics. In a few short years, Bob had become a world-renowned choreographer when he did Peggy Fleming's programs. Mom, at Carlo's urging, took Mrs. Fleming up on her offer. Doris picked me up from the airport, I stayed at her lovely home, and she drove me to the Culver City Rink to work with Bob Paul. No one asked her to do this for me. She offered to do it because of her love of skating, Carlo, Bob Paul, and maybe me, too. No one in the USFSA suggested it. I don't even know if Peggy knew. What an amazing gesture. I don't know if kindhearted Doris ever understood the impact that trip made on me. I hope so! She wanted to help a younger skater do well, like Peggy had. Peggy had made it and she was a star, headlining Ice Follies and in her own television specials. Mrs. Fleming, because of her unique experience as someone who had guided her own daughter to Olympic gold, knew exactly what to do to help another skater and I respected her for it. I remember reading newspaper articles about their struggles during Peggy's competitive days. I think mothers naturally tend to fight harder for their children's welfare than anyone else and I want to believe that mothers are now respected in the world of skating. It's hard for me to know, since I'm not a mother in the sport.

The mothers were never given transportation or lodging at international events. Many times, the skaters would be picked up at bus stops and the moms would be left standing, watching their children go off in a foreign land and trusting that they would be taken care of. It's understandable, feeling invisible and dismissed, that my mother began drinking in the afternoons. She did it in private and the other moms never did anything about it because they were not aware. The few male officials who befriended her, like Hugh Graham and Franklin Nelson, another wonderfully fair man, didn't know what my mother was up against. They respected her and were always so supportive. They were the reason that my mom kept fighting.

Being made to feel like a second-class citizen was not the cause of her discontent. But it certainly fueled her anger and depression. She had been thrust into the figure-skating world, kicking and screaming, and she could never accept it for what it was. I can't blame her. Even though the USFSA loved to produce its ice princesses, it remained a male-run organization. It was a different feeling in Canada, where the president of the Canadian Figure Skating Association was a woman. The Canadians were more progressive, both artistically and in a socially conscious context.

I was beginning to understand Mom's combative nature toward certain officials, but I could never understand why she couldn't seem to accept me. Nothing I did made her happy or proud. It was becoming more painful to me that my mother never seemed to enjoy being my mother. Very little had changed since the day I had landed my first double flip and yearned to get her approval, but instead received a harsh, "The other girls jump higher." I was now second in the nation, and fourth in the world, and still that wasn't good enough for her. Maybe she knew that that would be my incentive to keep striving!

What did have to change was my pattern of switching coaches. Somehow, my parents and I maneuvered my training at just the right time to just the right coach. And each coach had given me what I needed to succeed in reaching the next level. I changed coaches, on average, every two years, and by this point, I had been with Carlo more than two years. There were times in those two years when my mom went back home and I stayed in Denver without her. Once, when I was sixteen, my friend Lynn Grimditch (sister to Wayne, the world-champion ski jumper) came out and stayed with me for part of the summer. But it was during those times when Mom was gone that I felt my training was most lacking. I received less attention from Carlo when she was gone. I called her once, very worried, asking, "Don't I get any lessons?" because a week had gone by without any lessons from him. I was suspicious that my parents weren't paying their bills from Carlo. But that wasn't the case. Dad never let his bill run up and paid it every month.

I felt overdue for a change because we were accustomed to picking up and moving on every two years. But there was no one else higher on the coaching ladder than Carlo. No one else had the international cachet this man had. We had to make it work with Carlo, no matter what.

Carlo was not like Gus Lussi, who was a very demanding coach. Carlo was much more easygoing. He didn't push me. He trained skaters at an elite level and expected them to motivate themselves. He did wonders for my figures. He actually made me appreciate them. I started to practice them correctly once I began to break bad habits I had developed. I still had some of the bizarre techniques taught by Lussi, where I was twisted like a pretzel trying to do clean turns. Carlo also realized that my eyesight was far from 20/20 and that I needed glasses. Once I got those big-rimmed glasses, a whole new world opened up for me. I could suddenly see colors. They had been muted for me my entire life. Most importantly for my skating, I was able to see my tracings clearly and I could actually line up my circles. It was a wonder I had done figures as well as I had. I had passed all my tests so quickly that I never had a chance to develop a solid foundation in figures. With Carlo, I realized I had a respectable talent for figures and had not reached my potential. I began to understand that, with some work, I could really improve my reputation in figures and they wouldn't be such a weakness in my skating. Just as I had once been obsessed with perfecting my jumps and spins, I became obsessed with perfecting my circles, turns, and tracings. If I didn't get these right, there'd be no Olympics in my future.

Unfortunately, I felt I was becoming stagnant in free skating. I wasn't improving and learning new things the way I had while I was with Gus Lussi. I was getting frustrated and taking it out on my mother. Every mother-daughter relationship faces challenges in the teenage years, and ours was heightened not only by the pressures of skating but the isolation we felt. My temper flared out on the ice several times a session. If I didn't land a jump, I kicked the ice with the heel of my blade and left huge chunks of ice spinning in my wake. If I started my program and fell on the first jump, I'd sit on the ice and not get up while my music kept playing.

When I look back on this time, I realize I was acting like a temperamental spoiled brat. Once, Carlo snatched my record from the turntable and flung it across the ice like a Frisbee. He'd yell at me, calling me lazy. I was not stimulated. I was not inspired. Days would go by and I would not feel like being out on the ice. This disinterest was disturbing to me because I had never felt it before. Carlo found a way to blame my mother for my lack of motivation. Sometimes a practice session would be going fine and then she would walk in and my behavior would change completely. He told her not to come to the rink. She didn't take that demand lying down and fought back. She told him that when she wasn't there I didn't get the attention I needed.

Confirming her suspicions, Mrs. Nightingale, Lynn's mother, told my mom that when her daughter, Canada's darling, came to town, "Carlo doesn't teach Dorothy." Mom would go back to the apartment and have a nip to deal with the emotion of being shut out of her own child's future by a man she didn't trust. She knew Carlo wasn't training me hard enough, but she had no control over me. She hated that he didn't make me do a complete run-through of my program every single day. Carlo couldn't make me — I had to want to do it. Mom was absolutely right about having to do the run-throughs, but I was a rebellious teenager who was never going to agree with my mother. The person who was supposed to love me the most unconditionally was the same person who was most critical of me. I felt my mother was discouraging me and that took the love out of skating for me. It was only passion that fueled my energy for the sport. And my passion was disappearing.

Mom and I argued about everything. It seemed everything she did embarrassed me. She was bossing me around like I was still a little kid and I hated it. I even told her I hated her and she should leave me alone. I don't know how she put up with me. Most parents would have walked away from this awful situation. She dealt with it the only way she knew: self-medicating with alcohol. After all, she knew I couldn't survive without her. Teenagers don't understand these things. After Carlo would speak his mind at the rink, he was able to walk away, impervious to the damage he had done to my mother and me. He wasn't our family and wasn't emotionally involved. Carlo did his job — I was the one who needed the "iron fist." I was simply another one of his students. If I wasn't willing to do the work, he couldn't do it for me. Unfortunately, my mother and I never found relief from our growing divisiveness.

My mom would look for relief in the form of diversions, not only for me but also for her. She'd drive me out to Vail, about a hundred miles away. We weren't allowed to ski, but it was a beautiful spot and we both loved nature. She took me up to Sun Valley, Idaho, when I was invited to skate in one of their shows. Their famous outdoor rink lifted my spirits. Skating in the sunshine evoked a time in my life when skating was new and innocent, when I'd go to the ponds near my home in Riverside: if only it could be that way all the time. My mother went out of her way to help other skating families, lending a hand to move them into an apartment, shuttling them to the airport, or running any sort of errand. She was nice to anyone who was friendly to her. Why couldn't she be as nice to me? And when she was, why couldn't I see it?

The issues plaguing me in Denver increased in intensity when I won Nationals in Providence in 1974. The stakes were now raised by my Senior Ladies national champion status. Talk began to swirl that I could be the next Olympic ladies champion in two years. But only some people were aware of the turmoil I was experiencing. I was dealing with the hormonal mood swings of teenagedom, a family who was sacrificing their last dime to keep me here, and a mother too clinically depressed to find any happiness in my success. It's no wonder that I had an emotional moment of discomposure right on the ice at Worlds. Just before my turn to perform, the crowd began to boo. The event was in Munich, Germany, and I didn't know the crowd was supporting their German skater. They announced my name and the boos got louder and louder. So I thought it was because of me! I broke down in tears and skated off the ice. My father took me in his arms and comforted me. I didn't know what was going on. I went back out on the ice to get my guards and some in the crowd must have seen how upset I was. Suddenly, the booing turned to cheers. It was then that I realized the crowd had not been booing me, but the marks for the previous skater. I took a deep breath, composing myself, and took the ice for my program. I skated well enough to earn the silver medal, second to Christine Errath of East Germany. Carlo Fassi had seen to it that the international judges had validated my improvement in figures and accorded me the score that, after winning the free skating, kept me at the top; but I still needed true inspiration.

We thought we'd find it in off-ice training. I began heavy-duty athletic training sessions, a field that was in its infancy compared with today. So much is known today in the field of sports science, but we were clueless back then. There was little understanding of what kind of cross training a figure skater might benefit from. The idea then was that if strong muscles made me jump high, then stronger muscles would make me jump even higher. The philosophy was "more is better." So I was put on an exercise bike for hours, three times a week, with a very heavy load. The weight of the load was increased every week. We didn't know in those days that our bodies need time to repair. I began to get the largest set of thighs a figure skater could have. I wrapped them in Saran wrap, then put on my skating tights in the hope that the "fat" would be sweated off. Of course, it wasn't fat. I was building muscle. My skating became sluggish. The added muscle mass made me so tired.

I was lucky to have a good body type for skating. I never grew too much in any given year, unlike some skaters who grew so fast that they lost their timing for jumps. My hips and breasts didn't blossom so curvaceously that they got in the way of my movement. Athletes are always concerned about being at optimum weight, and my heavy thighs were depressing me. I was so exhausted that my mom thought maybe I had mononucleosis. It was all I could do to get through one day at a time. Luckily, Carlo realized the office training wasn't helping, but rather, was hurting me, especially my agility. He put an end to it and Mom quickly agreed — she saw it too. I began to jump higher and have more energy within a week.

In 1975, I won Nationals again, this time at the Oakland Coliseum in California. Then, at Worlds, I won the silver again, this time losing to Diane DeLeeuw from the Netherlands. Ironically, Diane had been an American skater, but because the field of skaters was so strong in her home state of California, she chose to represent the Netherlands, and was able to because of her mother's dual citizenship. I don't think my performances were lackluster, but it was becoming harder for me to focus. There were weeks in my training when I was physically and mentally burned out. So many of the skaters I knew who were my age were going into college or joining ice shows. I had the feeling that they were moving on with their lives and I wasn't. The Denver Ice Arena became a lonelier place. I felt like I was a trained seal, just going through the motions. Physically, I was wiped out. The pressure of the Olympics in less than a year was almost too much to bear.

I now realize that these physical and mental symptoms were warning signs of my own depression. But back then I had no idea. All I knew was that I was committed to going to the Olympics, no matter what — I just had to work and hang in there. I knew I had the ability. I just had to skate my best and I knew everything would fall into place. I had the dream that I could win the Olympics. But how was I going to get there with a coach who didn't believe in me, a mother who was at odds with us both, and a father too far away to do anything about it?

5
THIS WAY TO THE OLYMPICS

Nationals were held at the Broadmoor in 1976, the Olympic year. I kept my crown as the U.S. ladies figure skating champion, but I didn't feel I'd earned it. It was a hollow victory when I received marks I felt I didn't deserve. Linda Fratianne, at only fourteen years old, skated better than I and probably should have won. She had triples and I didn't. My double Axel was a fleeting jump, as always. Linda was the future of skating and I was the present. But I wasn't performing. I was ill-prepared. I didn't receive high scores, but I was still kept in first place because the USFSA knew I was still the U.S. favorite overseas. The best thing I had going for me, beside my drastic improvement in figures, were my programs, set to music discovered and cut together by my father. All the pieces were by the composer Erich Wolfgang Korngold from the themes of Errol Flynn movies, *Captain Blood, The Sea Hawk,*

Between Two Worlds, and *Escape Me Never.* The music had a lush, romantic sound that was very different from the other skaters' music. There was a majesty and a romance to it that captivated me.

With my close win, I suddenly was the underdog for the Olympics. Worse, I'd be up against the Eastern judging bloc. Even Carlo didn't believe in me anymore and was fed up with my antics, lack of motivation, and rebellion. He left for the European championships with John Curry, leaving me in Colorado with no coach. And it was less than a month before the Olympics.

My mom freaked out. We drove seventy miles back to Denver without a clue as to what the next step should be. The Denver rink was empty. There was no one there. My mom made frantic calls from our apartment to find a coach. She called her friend Ann Gram, who had been a knowledgeable confidante since the early Lake Placid years. Ann suggested we go to Peter Burroughs on Long Island. It meant I could live at home. My mom and I had always liked Peter. He was a gentleman and treated her with respect. My mother had an innate sense of which people in our lives were of high character and Mr. Burroughs was definitely one of them. She phoned him and told him our dilemma. He said, "Bring Dorothy here. I'll take care of her." Mom packed up our apartment and had us out of Denver within twenty-four hours. We flew home and I spent the night in my own bed for the first time in five years. I was overcome with emotion at being back in the bedroom I'd had as a little girl. I remembered life as it was when I had first started skating, just a little girl who loved ice skating completely and without question. Now, if I could just remember that feeling on the ice during training sessions! I felt broken down. But I saw the light at the end of tunnel.

As a practical matter, my first question to Mr. Burroughs was, "Will I have clean ice for figures?" Clean ice meant that I would be able to replicate the competition experience by not being able to see the tracings laid down before me in a previous patch. Even after resurfacing, it was usually possible to see these tracings through the thin layer of new ice. Having these tracings was beneficial and a hindrance at the same time. If the tracings were good, we used those marks and followed them. But it almost felt like cheating. If they were bad, it distracted us. Either way, they prevented the development of one's own skills in creating circles on blank ice. I would get to competition and my right-footed circles would be larger than my left-footed circles. Like most skaters, I didn't have the same control on my left side that I did on my right, so I developed the habit of making these circles too quickly. I knew I needed to have a clean sheet, the same as I would at the Olympics. Too many times in Denver, we did not have fresh ice. Peter was stunned. He said of course I would.

Peter Burroughs made me go through both my short and long program every single day without stopping. If I fell, I couldn't start the program from the beginning. No, I had to get up and keep going through the program, because this could very well happen in competition. I had to learn to get up quickly and carry on. And I definitely couldn't continue my rotten habit of kicking the ice. He was strict, demanding, and a perfectionist. He was exactly what I needed. He knew my personality and didn't put up with childish behavior. My mom didn't have to be in the arena to watch over me: She could trust that Peter Burroughs was doing the job. Besides, the country was in the middle of a gas shortage and she had to wait in line for hours to fill up the tank to haul me around.

Peter didn't allow me to play the games I had with Carlo. I couldn't get away with it. I was working very hard and beginning to feel prepared, the feeling I'd once had years before. Most importantly, I began to feel my passion and determination reignited.

Mom appealed to the USFSA to designate Peter Burroughs as my Olympic coach. She didn't trust that Carlo would be an attentive coach in Innsbruck. Her request was refused. They insisted that Carlo remain my coach on record. It was decided Carlo had been my coach for five years and that was the way it should be. Besides, the international judges would not look kindly at my abrupt change. As it stood, I was considered an underdog, by my own admission and by my own country.

There was so much excitement and activity leading up to the Olympics, but compared to the pressure on today's athletes, it was nothing. First, there was an exhibition in New Jersey to help raise funds for the team. Then it was off to Rockefeller Center for a press conference and fittings for our Olympic gear. I had my picture taken for *Time* magazine. They told me it might be a cover story, but that if another world event were more important, it wouldn't be. Somehow it made the cover.

The night before I left for Europe, I had my hair cut by the world-famous hairstylist, Suga. I had always hated my short hair.

There was one time when I was younger when I'd grown it longish and I'd enjoyed it, but it was easier to keep it short — "wash 'n' wear hair." I had read about Suga in magazines and wanted him to cut my hair. I was aware of his masterful talent after seeing the chic haircut he gave Melissa Militano, the pairs skater who was also in Senior Ladies with me. My dad had written him a letter, asking him if he could cut my hair for the Olympics. He graciously agreed to do it, staying very late at his shop. Of course, I had no idea that this wedge style would become so famous. I just thought if I had to have short hair anyway, I might as well have something fashionable.

I had never competed in an Olympics before and this was certainly going to be very different from anything I had ever experienced. The media were paying lots of attention to us. It was interesting — I had been number two in the world for two years in a row, but there hadn't really been any press interest. Suddenly, the eyes of the world were on us and every country in the world wanted a five-minute interview. It was wild, but not like it is today. It was 1976, four years prior to the U.S. hockey team's victory that woke up our country to the huge appeal of the Winter Olympics. Our nation related more closely to the Summer Olympics, because it involved sports widely played in the United States. Most people had ridden a bike, learned how to swim, or dribbled a basketball down a court. But few had sailed down a mountainside in a bobsled, soared off a ninety-meter ski jump, or been cast into the air in a throw double Axel. Thus, the United States did not fund winter sports at all. They really didn't recognize winter sports, although skiing did have a strong sponsorship base from private sources.

Our team uniforms were horrible. I don't mean to sound ungrateful, but they were ugly and impractical. We were given short plastic boots, a polyester suit unsuitable for winter, suitcases whose clasps would not close, and coats so puffy and cumbersome we looked like Pillsbury Doughboys. We could barely walk in them as we entered the stadium for the opening ceremonies. The West Germans had stylish and warm clothing designed by the famous skier Willy Bogner. The Russians had luscious sable coats, and the Italians had chic white wool coats and rich leather boots. There is a custom of athletes trading their Olympic gear with other countries to obtain long-lasting mementos of their time spent with the best athletes from all over the world. But no other country would trade with us. They didn't want our things. We were still the underdogs of the international winter sports world. When I look back at the '76 Olympics, as compared with today's, I think maybe we were lucky. Today, there is so much more media pressure on the athletes. I didn't have that. We weren't even televised live. The lack of hype surrounding the event was definitely a plus for me. I didn't know going in that it would change my life forever if I won. Had I known, I probably would have choked.

The U.S. Olympic figure skating team was set up to practice in Garmisch, West Germany, for the week leading up to the opening ceremonies. This helped us adjust to the European time change, their food, their water, and their different training conditions. We were housed in a small *pensione* in town and were grateful for the extra two hours of practice ice. Innsbruck wasn't available for practice, and ice time at the nearby rink was limited to one hour a day. I met up with Carlo in Garmisch. He had probably heard that my mother had tried to get Peter to be my Olympic coach, but he seemed so genuinely happy to see me that my heart melted and I completely forgot about his apparent abandonment three weeks prior. I felt that his favorite was John Curry, but once the men's event was over, I knew I would have Carlo's undivided attention.

Carlo suggested I might want to stay in a hotel, because Peggy Fleming had chosen not to stay in the Grenoble Olympic Village when she had competed in 1968 and that had obviously worked to her advantage. But I didn't want to do the same. I wanted to be in the Olympic Village. It was thrilling to be with the other athletes. The Olympic Village was our own oasis, away from coaches, parents, judges, and the media. It was so clean, with no smoking and no alcohol. It was comforting to know that all the other athletes, no matter their sport, were under the same pressures. And it was great fun eating in the cafeteria together. I always had an "Olympic" appetite — I could eat a whole box of cereal for breakfast — and it was fun to see others eating far more than I did. I determined that if all other competitions had been set up like the Olympics, I certainly would have loved competing all these years. Without judges around, we could be ourselves. The other athletes were not critical; they were just going about their daily routine. Skaters were judged when they were off the ice as much as when they were on. So it was refreshing to focus only on skating.

While training in Garmisch, I came down

with a fever. History was repeating itself. Just as when I had become so sick before the 1972 Nationals, another crucial time in my competitive career, I had to fight the flu at this critical time. My mother watched my practices, and I could tell by her reaction that I wasn't skating well. I placed second in the figures. That seemed to make everyone around me nervous. The assumption was that I was going to end up with a silver medal again, the same place as in the prior two world championships.

Then miracle of miracles! I scored a perfect 6.0 in my short program and moved into first place. Now it was a matter of being able to hold on to first. I felt the pressure become even more intense. It was Thursday, and we had an early morning practice the day before we skated our long programs. Mom had made plans to get me far away from the rink and my competitors, knowing that I should get my mind off what was going to happen on Friday. We all needed a distraction from the intensity of the pressure. She scheduled the entire family to go on the "*Sound of Music* Tour," two hours away in Salzburg. My father, Marcia, Sandy, and my sister-in-law, "Perky," had arrived to join in the festivities. The Olympic Committee gave Mom and Dad a difficult time about my leaving their sight. Mom stood firm, and she and the rest of the family drove to Salzburg while Dad and I hopped on the train after my morning practice.

I was a huge Julie Andrews fan and still obsessed with *The Sound of Music.* We visited the glorious cathedral where Maria and Captain von Trapp were married, the gazebo where they'd filmed "I Am Sixteen Going on Seventeen," and the exterior of the von Trapp mansion. This diversion served the same purpose as those miniature-golf courses my parents had found over the years. I reminisced about earlier times. I could see the light at the end of the tunnel, which was thrilling and frightening at the same time. The song "Edelweiss" plays a central role in the musical and it had played a central role in my life when Gus Lussi had encouraged me to skate to it. When I'd skated to the song at Madison Square Garden when I was twelve, I had felt such happiness using the program I'd created mostly on my living room floor. It's still one of my favorite songs. Hearing the song "Edelweiss" again, in the hills that were the actual setting of the movie, I felt the same inspiration that I had when I was twelve and creating moves to this beautiful piece of music. More than a decade of a tough climb in such a competitive sport had almost erased the beauty of that "Edelweiss" moment. But now, the feeling was evoked once again, and it carried me through my final performance at the Olympics. My mom had known just what to do.

Carlo had advised me at our U.S. Olympic practice sessions at Garmisch that I was to see how I felt during my run-throughs. I had two double Axels in my long program and it was essential for me to land both in order to have a chance of winning. My double Axels had different setups. The first one I did after a Wally jump, and it was not a difficult entry for me: I didn't have too much time to over-think it and it was fairly consistent. The second one was more difficult. It came three minutes into the program, when my legs would start to feel fatigued and begin to burn. At that point, I usually started to feel winded.

Fortunately, with the training I had done, I wasn't feeling the weakness that I sometimes felt during practice. As much as the jump terrified me, I went for it and landed it. I was so excited that I didn't even attempt the double toe loop. Next came my footwork, and then, in the last thirty seconds, after I did my Russian split, I stepped forward and almost lost my balance. No one seemed to notice. I went into my Hamill Camel and then my final scratch spin. I finished, and the applause was deafening. Flowers rained down on the ice, thrown toward me in the European tradition that had begun with bullfighters in Spain.

I skated off the ice and into my father's arms. I squinted to try to see my marks because I didn't wear my glasses for free skating. What a relief to be finished. Now it was out of my hands. There were several more skaters. They were my toughest competitors, and I sat to watch them skate. Diane DeLeeuw of the Netherlands and Christine Errath of East Germany both had been world champions and I had never won Worlds. I looked to find Mom in the stands, but that was fruitless because of my poor eyesight. I didn't think much about it because I assumed she was there with Marcia, Sandy, and Perky. I just couldn't find them in the crowd. After all the skaters were finished, the unofficial standings came in. But we had to wait for the official results. We were escorted to "doping control" for drug testing. Urinating into a cup was standard procedure after an athlete's competitive performance, and I found it amusing. Three of us sitting in a room, drinking water, orange juice, anything so we could leave our specimen. But when skaters are nervous, we pee every couple of minutes, so by the time we've warmed up and performed, there's no fluid left in our bodies. Meanwhile, my father, a master mathematician, was tallying up the scores by hand. I was in "doping" for two hours because I had nothing left to urinate. They finally gave me beer to get what they needed.

When I came back, my father and Carlo had figured I had won. My dad held up one finger to indicate first place, gave me a proud grin, and winked. He also spotted Marcia, Sandy, and Perky in the audience. These were the days before computers and the instantaneous display of placements on a scoreboard. Naturally, I wanted to believe my dad's tally, but I still wanted to wait for the official announcement. Then the ABC announcer, Chris Schenkel, gave me a wink and a nod. We couldn't hear that ABC was announcing to the world that I had won. The red carpet was rolled onto the ice and the podium was carried out as officials gathered. It was all happening so quickly. I found out that I won when the live audience learned, as the medals were announced.

Immediately after our national anthem was played and I was surrounded by well-wishers, I looked around again for Mom.

"Where's Mom?" I asked Dad.

"She's back at the hotel," he hesitantly answered.

I remembered the last thing she had said to me: "I'll see you later." It was then that I realized she had not come to see me skate. She had been at the hotel the whole time.

When we walked into that hotel room and found my mother in a cloud of cigarette smoke, her face looked pale, her voice was weak, and her hands were trembling. She looked as if she'd seen a ghost. All those years, her behavior had mystified me. I still try to rationalize it. Here we are thirty years later, and afraid of what she might answer, I still haven't had the guts to ask her why she didn't come to the arena that day. It was up to me to learn more about my mother as I matured, to find the answer for myself. But at that time, I felt she didn't want me to win, that she didn't believe in me, and that she really didn't care! Dad had called her the moment he thought I had won, but she'd said there wasn't enough time for her to make it over for the medal ceremony. There was no transportation once the event was over. She didn't have a ticket to get in because she'd given hers to my sister-in-law. The arena was small and the security was tight. The sad thing was she was the person most responsible for me being up there on top of that podium, and no one even asked where she was.

Truthfully, I think she was just plain exhausted. Burned out from all the years of having to be my everything — my seamstress, my cook, my chauffeur, my negotiator, my manager, my scheduler, my bill-payer, my decision-maker, and my line of defense. From having to encourage me by doing so much for me, but not let me become conceited. Really, all she had wanted to do was to be my mother. It was a Herculean task to fight through the world of figure skating and to help me excel in it. She had sacrificed herself for my dream. But I was too young and too eager to appreciate that when I won the Olympics. Maybe she felt she was doing me a favor by not being in the arena because Carlo claimed she made me nervous. She was relieved when my dad showed up in Innsbruck and told her he would go to the practices and the events with me. Carlo and my dad had a mutual respect for each other. That's why it looked to the worldwide audience watching on television that my dad was the sole parent sharing my glory. It was classic "good cop, bad cop." My dad got to be the good cop. I was so disappointed Mom wasn't there because I wanted her to share the experience, whether or not I won. She, more than anyone, knew what it had taken. I was proud of my Olympic performance. I was well prepared and the confidence of training hard had paid off. It was the culmination of my hard work, and the love, sacrifice, tenacity, and perseverance of so many people since I had first stepped on the ice at eight years old. *Yes, I wanted my mom to be there.*

There was a reception for the U.S. team that night, which Mom did attend. Dick Button pulled me aside and gave me a prized bottle of champagne. Marcia and I escaped into a bathroom. We looked at each other and said, "Olympic champion," then screamed at the top of our lungs, stomping our feet like little kids. Marcia had also sacrificed to get me here, and we were so happy we could share in the joy together. Marcia was always supportive. I always felt her genuine happiness for my successes. And we would often commiserate about our relationships with Mom. We both craved her acceptance and approval.

Meanwhile, outside at the reception, Ben Wright, one of the U.S. judges, approached my parents and said, "What's this? I hear Dorothy's not going to Worlds."

My mom exploded at him. "That has not been decided!"

Of course I wanted to compete in Worlds. I had yet to win a world title. My mom was defending me, as she always had. My mother suspected that Carlo had planted the idea of my not competing, just as he had four years prior, when Julie Lynn Holmes had decided to retire from amateur competition after the Olympics. Worlds are always scheduled after the Olympics. Now the USFSA, or Carlo, had determined that my time was done and they were busy catapulting the next American ice princess onto the international stage. My mom wasn't going to let them plot a world title out of my reach.

Then Mom chose to throw them another curveball. The world team was traveling to Helsinki, Finland, to train for Worlds in Gothenburg, Sweden. I was expected to be there with them. Instead, Mom and I took a detour. She wanted me to have a couple of days off from the eight-hour training schedule. Trixie Schuba, the 1972 Olympic champion from Austria, arranged for us to see my first opera, *Madame Butterfly,* at the venerable Vienna State Opera House. We had box seats and stayed at the Imperial Palace, possibly the most luxurious hotel in the world. We went to a Vienna tea and the orchestra played "The Skater's Waltz" when they saw me. It was a blissful time: My mom and I had a wonderful two days in Vienna. On the train ride up to Helsinki, the exhaustion from the Olympics finally set in, and as I was falling asleep on my mother's lap, I heard a nun who was sitting across from us recognize me.

"I saw your daughter skate on TV. She did so beautifully."

"Yes, she did," my mother answered.

"She must be tired."

"Yes, she is."

My mom let me sleep. She let no one disturb me. On that train ride, we had a rare and precious moment as mother and daughter. It felt right, so comforting, so warm and relaxing. Our dream had been achieved. I felt happy, fulfilled, serene, and worry-free. I think Mom felt the same way. I think all she wanted was to have me to herself, if only for this brief time. She must have known that, with my win, I would soon be separated from her. And then something happened at Worlds, my final amateur competition, that symbolized the fact that I'd better grow up fast.

Over the years, beginning when I had started competing, I had grown a collection of small stuffed animals that people had given me for luck. I'd kept them in my skate bag and the collection had grown to ten. No matter where I was, these dolls and animals had always made me feel at home. They reminded me of the nice people who had given them to me. One was a koala bear, another was a monkey, and another was a rubber troll from the Wormser family, who'd first enrolled me in competition at the Wollman rink. I set up this collection alongside the barrier during figures. All the other competitors knew about my collection. They were my little family, cheering me on, a source of security. I was superstitious about them being there. I had used them at the Olympics and they had obviously worked. But after the compulsory figures in Gothenburg, they disappeared! It was a sign that my childhood had come to an abrupt end.

Hollywood types were moving in, advising my family that I'd better turn professional right away, while I was "hot." I could have rested on my laurels, but I kept on training, getting up at the crack of dawn, because I was determined to be World Champion, too! I was told that I was taking a big risk by going on to Worlds. If I lost, it would tarnish my Olympic win, and if I won, people wouldn't know. But I knew what I wanted. At Worlds I skated well and won. It is the gold medal of which I am most proud.

After Worlds, the team members were expected to go on the International Skating Union exhibition tour with teams from all the other countries. The purpose of the tour was to raise money for international judges and for holding Worlds the following year. The skaters were allowed to be paid sixty dollars per performance. There was an older Russian skater to whom I became attracted on this tour. My mother had heard that he had a bad reputation with girls and didn't want me near him. She told me he was too old for me. To defy her, one night I took off alone with him in a cab, leaving her standing open-mouthed on the curb. The Russians had no control over their male skaters, and Carlo had very open European ideas about relationships, so my mom got no support for keeping me away from this man. Our next stop was the USSR. She feared my going there when I was so interested in this man and she had no control over me. Worse, the Russian man would be in his home country. She went to the Olympic Committee and asked to leave the tour, to return to the United States. She wanted to take me home. They refused. President Gerald Ford had invited me to the White House, and the Olympic Committee still refused.

Finally, my mom paid for the tickets herself, and we flew back home. I was amazed to learn I was being called "America's Sweetheart" because my Olympic win was on Friday the thirteenth and had been announced in the newspapers the next day, Valentine's Day. There was a parade in my honor in my hometown, and I forgot all about the Russian skater. I met Queen Elizabeth at a White House reception with President Ford. I had won the Olympics and there should have been a sense of great relief and celebration. One might think, and I certainly did, that all problems would dissolve in the wake of such an accomplishment.

But they were just beginning. And I was at the ripe old age of nineteen. I sure thought I was an adult. I had so much growing up to do and had no way of knowing I was now going to be fed to the wolves!

6
HOLLYWOOD, HERE I COME

The phone rang off the hook. My dad had flown ahead, home to Connecticut and back to work. Mostly he answered the calls: They were primarily from managers and agents who had tracked him down and wanted to represent me. I knew what I wanted, so I wondered what purpose an agent or manager would serve. I had wanted to skate with Shipstad and Johnson's Ice Follies since I was little. While I was growing up, they always had been the classiest of shows. They had the best costumes and the best choreography. I idolized the stars of the show, "Mr. Debonair" Richard Dwyer, the glamorous Karen Kresge, and the beautiful adagio team of Nancy and Leandre. I was invited backstage in Denver to visit with friends who had joined before me, like Atoy Wilson, and the dance team of Judy Schwomeyer and Jim Sladky, whom I knew from Lake Placid days. Carlo knew everybody behind the scenes in the show because Peggy Fleming had skated in it. Through him, I was able to meet the elegant Bob and Helen Maxson, who were the show's choreographers. I'd ask everybody questions — what they did with their free time, where they stayed, who they got to meet on the road, and how late they stayed up. I had been all over the world and skated in exhibitions in dozens of cities by this point, and I had always had so much fun. I assumed I'd have as much fun in Ice Follies.

At that time, the owner was Arthur Wirtz, an enormously successful businessman who also owned the Chicago Blackhawks. He flew my parents and me to Chicago to meet with him. Huge in physical stature, he intimidated me. Mr. Wirtz had owned *The Sonja Henie Hollywood Ice Review* in Madison Square Garden. His shows were lavish, and he was very proud of having worked with the great Sonja Henie. He sat behind the largest desk I'd ever seen and said Sonja did a hula number he always loved. He wanted me to learn how to do the hula. It quickly became apparent that Mr. Wirtz had never seen me skate. He had not seen my Olympic performance on television nor the world championship. Olympic figure skating and ice-show skating were completely different than in Sonja Henie's era. He had no idea what I was about. No idea of the athleticism I had tried to achieve in sports. No idea of the years I'd spent training for the Olympics. He wanted me to do the hula. I looked at him questioningly. He said, "Oh, it's easy. All you have to do is learn to move your hands. You'll get lots of curtain calls that way."

I felt so insulted. Times had changed, and he didn't realize it. I would have been laughed out of the sport if I had done what he had asked. My dream of joining the Ice Follies had been dashed — with a grass skirt.

George Eby, president of Ice Capades, took a different tactic. He came to see my family and me in Riverside and was a complete gentleman. He showed me respect. He was a "hands-on" president. He understood the demands of a top athlete and the need to have time for proper training and rehearsal. We agreed on the number of weeks I would skate each year. He agreed to a two-year contract with a third-year option. It would be the most lucrative contract signed by a female athlete up to that time.

But the numbers didn't mean anything to me. Thousands of dollars a week or a couple hundred, it was all the same to me because I had never had any before. Prior to signing my contract, the only money I had ever earned was from babysitting — where my going rate was two dollars an hour. But no amount of money was going to stave off the depression that set in after the Olympics. I had reached the Impossible Dream, a dream so unachievable that I was afraid to speak about it while I was working toward it. And somehow I did it. I should have been happy. But I was stunned by my true reaction. I suddenly felt directionless. I had no goal anymore. I didn't have another dream. I felt lost. My dream had come true and the only life I knew, training and competing, had come to an abrupt stop. What had replaced it were days, weeks, and months of business meetings. I was unaccustomed to sitting in on meetings: I didn't know what to say or how to say what I meant. My shyness and lack of confidence really showed. My parents and I were put in the position of trying to learn the business of entertainment overnight, because there were so many decisions to make. We met endlessly with lawyers, business managers, press agents, accountants, ice-show owners, and investment firms, just to name a few. We tried to weed out the companies that approached me to endorse products. ABC wanted to do TV variety specials, and we had to figure out who would negotiate those deals and who would produce them. There wasn't time to make mistakes. There was so much to be done. It was already April and rehearsals would begin with Ice Capades in June. We needed time to choose music, rehearse choreography, do costuming, finish a photo shoot for the programs, and develop public relations materials. This was a whole new world for me.

My parents tried their best to protect me, but they didn't know what they were doing either. It was an emotional and stressful time. There were too many lunches, dinners, fancy banquets, and first-class flights with heavy food. I still had my Olympic appetite, but I wasn't exerting energy to match it. I was sitting around at meetings. I wasn't training. I was burned out and emotionally drained. I couldn't concentrate. I wasn't happy. I should have been on top of the world, but I was ill-equipped to handle these new pressures. All I knew how to do was to get up every morning at 4 A.M. to go to the rink and practice. My day had always been planned around structured activity toward a specific goal I cared about. Suddenly, that was gone, and my present life was so hectic and without meaning. It was new and sometimes exciting, but I felt so incompetent. Of course, while I was training for the Olympics, it had occurred to me to wonder what I would do after the Olympics. I figured I would skate in a show for two years, then go back to school to become an interior designer. I really didn't have a role model to guide me. Peggy Fleming had been off the road, having her family. Billie Jean King had been a professional already when she hit it big. It was 1976. There were no professional teams in women's basketball. There was no woman in the world of golf I could look to for an example. The sports pages barely acknowledged figure skating as a sport. To the sports writers, who were primarily men, our competitions seemed frivolous. The cultural news pages didn't acknowledge the sport as art. And the entertainment pages didn't think the ice shows merited entertainment news. So I floundered in the middle, in a no-woman's land. It would be another sixteen years before athletes competing in the Olympics would be allowed to earn money — basketball's Dream Team inaugurated the new rules in the summer of 1992.

By the time I arrived in Los Angeles that summer to begin working with Ice Capades, I had gained fifteen pounds. It doesn't sound like much, but it was a lot for a five-foot-three skater. I was so heavy that one of the chorus boys commented, after being told by the choreographer that he had to skate around me, "If I have to skate around her, honey, you better call me a cab." My self-esteem was fragile enough. I didn't need to hear that. There was so much I had to learn. I had to take tap and jazz lessons with Roland Dupree. And I had to learn to speak into a microphone to the audience. Yikes! I know I must have appeared to be a lost cause to the seasoned professionals who were helping me. I was still so painfully self-conscious about my speaking ability; there was no way they were going to get me to talk to crowds of people every night. My decade of appearing in the shows of Lake Placid, Sun Valley, the Jimmy Fund, and the ISU tours could not have prepared me for the expectations of Ice Capades. Up until this point, show skating to me meant we could use vocals in our music. It was exhibition skating. Ice Capades was professional entertainment. I had to learn to be an entertainer, as well as remain an athlete.

George Eby quickly realized I was not going to become a glamour girl overnight. I was more work than anyone had realized. He teamed me up with Juanita Purcelly, a logical choice for many reasons. She was born into the famous Purcelly family of Germany, known for their circus tumbling. The family made the switch to ice shows when Juanita was a little girl, and she grew up in the show business of ice skating. She became an adagio pair skater and stayed on the road as an adult. There she met and married Gary Visconti when he turned pro and joined Holiday on Ice. Gary was my idol from competition. He had won the senior men's national title twice when I was just starting out, and competed in the '68 Olympics. Gary and Juanita left the road to raise their two daughters and settled in Los Angeles, where Gary coached amateur competitors. They had a lovely place on the West Side of Los Angeles and I lived with them during my first round of rehearsals.

Juanita was full of personality and energy, and had an outrageous sense of humor. I liked her immediately and intensely. Her job was to help me adjust to my new lifestyle. She became my new best friend, my chaperone, my dietician, and my glamour coach. She was Professor Higgins to my Eliza. I was like a "Fair Lady" who had to quickly grow up in a world for which I was totally unprepared. The show-business side of skating was strange enough, but even stranger for the likes of me. Juanita was more than capable of helping me find the right clothes, teaching me to apply stage makeup, and preparing me for the realities of show life. However, we were both unprepared for the role she would take on, almost inadvertently in the beginning, but brazenly later on. She became my second mother. Her surrogacy began when I met the love of my life, Dean Paul Martin.

I told Juanita about an incident that had happened earlier in the spring. My mother and I were in Los Angeles to sign my Ice Capades contract. We were staying at the Beverly Hills Hotel when I received a phone call from Desi Arnaz Jr. I had never met Desi and could not guess why he would be calling me. He said he had watched me win the Olympics, and I wondered how he'd tracked me down at the Beverly Hills Hotel. Apparently it was easy. His mom, Lucille Ball, and I had the same publicity agent. The agent knew I was in town for the closing night of Ice Capades, and Desi had gotten this information out of him somehow. Desi said his friend Dean had deduced that I was probably at one of two places, the Beverly Wilshire or the Beverly Hills Hotel. The young man was definitely persistent.

"Do you want to have a drink?" Desi asked.

"I'm going to see the Ice Capades tonight."

"Oh, we're going too." He meant his friend Dean Paul Martin and himself.

I thought that was a great coincidence, but said that I might see them there.

And I did see the two of them there. I was riding up on an escalator with George Eby and my new manager, Jerry Weintraub. I felt very comfortable around Jerry. He was young, hip, sincere, and didn't seem like what I had heard was stereotypical Hollywood. He represented three of my idols, John Denver, and Karen and Richard Carpenter, all of whom I felt were positive role models. Jerry spotted Desi and Dean on the escalator going down, and he pointed them out. I turned around and saw them. They waved and said hi. There was something sweet and adorable that struck me about Dean when I saw him for the first time.

I certainly had heard of the singing group Dino, Desi & Billy, as they were the teenage heartthrobs of the '60s. They had come to fame before any of them had yet turned fifteen. But I wasn't thinking about any of that when I saw them for that brief moment on the escalator. I was thinking, "Why would they want to come to an ice show?"

When I got back to the Beverly Hills Hotel, I fell asleep and was awakened by a phone call.

"How about that drink?"

"Who is this?"

"It's Desi. I just saw you at the show."

"Oh, hello. Again."

Of course, I was surprised to hear from him. And flattered. But I said I was very tired and had to fly back East the next day.

He asked if I would be returning to Los Angeles. I said I would be coming out later in the summer.

"Please give me a call when you come back." He gave me his phone number.

I had obviously been thinking about these phone calls from Desi and the chance meeting at the Sports Arena because I repeated the story to Juanita. I still had his phone number. She immediately jumped up, grabbed the phone, and shouted, "Call him!"

"I can't do that."

"Why not?"

"Because I've never done anything like it."

"You can do it now. This is the new Dorothy."

She dialed the number and made me talk to him.

"I'm back in town," I told Desi.

"Great. Let's get together. Do you mind if I bring a friend along?"

"No, that would be fine."

I didn't know whom he was going to bring.

But it felt less stressful if there were to be three of us.

The third person was Dean. We went to a restaurant on Canyon Drive called the Luau. Desi Jr. kept excusing himself to go talk to other people, leaving Dean and me to ourselves. Desi wasn't being rude: I suspected he was trying to get Dean and me alone together. Dean seemed as shy as I was. I learned he was an athlete, on tour with the ATP, the Association of Tennis Professionals. He was ranked 120th in the world. He knew the level of devotion required to become a great athlete and he respected the elite level I had achieved. I made the mistake of calling him Dino and he politely asked me not to use that nickname. "Dino" was in his past and he wanted to be called Dean. When Desi came back, he suggested we liven up the night so we went to a place called the Candy Store Disco. Again, Desi made himself scarce while we were at the disco, leaving Dean and me alone. He asked me to dance. He was a good dancer, while I, despite my early days dancing at the Marcy Hotel in Lake Placid, was always incredibly self-conscious on the dance floor. Thankfully, it was a slow dance, "Always and Forever," and we seemed to really hit it off. Although our childhoods had been so different, we still had so much in common. He was extremely funny. His sharp wit made me laugh all night. Yet he was also incredibly sweet. And he was devastatingly handsome. He told me how much he loved his young son, Alex, from his former marriage to the actress Olivia Hussey. I was intrigued that this young man was already a father. When Desi returned, he wasn't the least bit perturbed by his friend moving in on me. And he seemed quite happy that Dean and I had set another date. Dean never mentioned to me that he had asked Desi to help him set up a date with me. He would never admit it. But it was clear to me that he thought he needed his friend's help and support to reel me in.

Juanita was overjoyed that Dean and I were smitten with each other. My mom sneered her disapproval. She didn't want me getting involved with what she called "Hollywood types." She liked the idea of Dean even less because it didn't seem to her that he had a real job.

My first paycheck from Ice Capades went to my parents to pay years of back taxes they owed, totaling over $100,000. I also bought them a new car, which they desperately needed. I was so proud to be able to do this for my mom and dad. I did these things willingly and with gladness in my heart. They deserved it. They had not been able to pay the taxes because of skating. They had driven old, unreliable cars because of me. I now had an accountant, and I expressed to my dad that I'd like Mom to have a regular weekly allowance so that she would always have money in her purse. The hurt and guilt I felt at seeing my mother go hungry so that I could eat was still very vivid to me. I hated how she had to go begging to Dad for money. Little did I know, there had always been an argument about it.

My parents set up their own company, Riverside Management Services, to handle the monthly income from my checks. They were still doing work for me, handling any fan mail that came to the house and sending out pictures, even though I had an assistant to take care of that. Jerry Weintraub suggested that I transfer my money to California. My parents wanted me to keep my money with the people they had found for me in New York City. I followed Jerry's lead, working with his lawyer. My parents felt threatened when my money left Connecticut, although I continued sending them a monthly income. They thought they could control me if I stayed on the East Coast. But my new life was starting in California. I trusted Jerry. And I trusted Juanita. She knew about this new world of entertainment I was in, while my parents and I were clueless.

My mom continued to dislike Dean, even though she still wasn't taking the time to get to know him. She believed he wasn't good for me. We had a huge fight in which she ripped a string of pearls off of my neck: The pearls bounced all over the floor, and most of them were lost. The pearls were a gift from the Crown Prince of Japan. He had given them to me when I'd skated in the Pre-Olympics in 1971. I had kept them all these years and wore them for special occasions. Dean knew how important they were to me. When he learned that my mom had broken them, he bought me a new pearl necklace and sweetly gave it to me as a Christmas present. I still have them and I wear it often. I treasure them.

Juanita was so supportive of my dating Dean that she came with me on our second and third dates so she could make sure they went well. I was so insecure that we both thought Dean might get the wrong message from me. The first date was at Hamburger Hamlet on Sunset Boulevard. The second date was at the restaurant Dan Tana's, where I used my American Express card for the first time and Juanita had to show me how to sign for a dinner.

It was natural and easy for me to shift my allegiance from my mother to Juanita because Juanita was telling me everything I needed and wanted to hear. She was becoming more to me than just a mentor showing me the ropes. There were so many characteristics of Juanita that were similar to my mother's, although I didn't see it at the time. Juanita was devoted to me. She was caring and nurturing. She was a focused person who knew what to do and how to get there. But she was also headstrong, domineering, and controlling.

Excitement was building toward the opening night of Ice Capades in Pittsburgh on September 15, 1976. Jerry Weintraub flew in with Karen Carpenter. She and I had become good friends. My mother ran into Jerry backstage. He was full of anticipation, but my mother dashed his visions of a successful opening by proclaiming, "She's going to go out there and fall on her face because she hasn't been training!"

My mother, as she has been so many times, was right. I had not been training: My time on the ice had been spent rehearsing routines with other cast members, not in jumping and spinning drills. But lack of practice was the least of my problems that night. I fell twice and I was only in two numbers. The first number, I fell on a double Axel. The second time, my blade got stuck on a coin from one of the costumes, and it took me three tries to stand upright. Then I had to maneuver around duck droppings. There was a magician in the show who turned a rabbit into a duck at the end of his act. Every time the magician had grabbed the duck to put him back in his cage, the poor thing had gotten scared and pooped on the ice. For the first time, a paying public was getting a look at me and this was what they got. I had only skated under pristine conditions when I competed. The ice was always perfect. The disappointment of the audience was echoed in the terrible press I received after my professional debut. The headlines also screeched about how uncomfortable I was with a microphone. I received pity telegrams from other entertainers who claimed they had also blown their opening nights. John Denver, probably prompted by Jerry Weintraub, sent me one telling me not to worry. Things would get better. Sure they would, if I could practice more and if excrement and bits of costumes could get cleaned off the ice before I skated. But that wasn't going to happen. I was in the circus now, sharing the spotlight with variety acts, and somehow I had to adjust.

It was up to me and only me to take my skating seriously. There was no one on the road to whom I could turn to inspire me. The show people had little understanding of the training hours necessary to perform at an Olympic level. It was unrealistic to expect that I could repeat my Olympic performance night after night, show after show, three times on Saturday and twice on Sunday. I was lucky to have done it once in Innsbruck. Yet I was expected to, by the audience, by my new employers, and by the cast and crew. Nobody saw the years of hard work it had taken me to get onto that podium in Innsbruck. They only saw the end result. The backstage crew used to poke fun at me warming up on the tiny bit of ice available backstage while they moved sets and props on and off. They had never seen anybody try to warm up so intensely. They had been on the road for years, and I was an oddity to them. It wasn't much easier with the other skaters. The older chorus girls resented me because I had my own dressing room. Still, I loved all the show people: We were really one huge family. Mostly, they were hardworking, career performers living out of trunks delivered city to city.

Juanita, who grew up with these people,

could not travel with me to every city. She had family obligations. So I asked my best friend since third grade, Kim Danks, to come on the road with me. She was my traveling companion and assistant. She and I were able to stay best friends all those years because her family treated me like one of their own. Even though I was gone so much we had kept up communication by writing letters. She always let me know her schedule so I could get her on the phone. When we'd see each other, it was like we had never been apart. I will always be grateful to her for coming on the road with me, because she became my touchstone. She was not a skater and her perspective helped to keep me levelheaded as we struggled through my jampacked days. Neither one of us knew what we were doing. My mom was ensconced back in her life in Connecticut. She had retrenched herself with old friends, bowling and playing bridge with them, and seemed happy to be relieved of the pressure of my demanding life.

The pressure placed on me was different from that on the other soloists in the show. My Olympic medal was the big draw, and in each city I had to do numerous interviews, in addition to press conferences during the day. It was fatiguing and separated me from the other skaters, who were either sleeping, resting by the pool, or out having fun somewhere else. Worse, my fear of speaking in front of people had not abated just because I'd had an Olympic medal placed around my neck. I had no idea what to say and I didn't understand why people would be interested in what I had to say. I was just a reserved, naïve, clueless girl who had lived her whole life in an icebox. I may have seemed sure of myself, but I was anything but. My one constant was that I loved to skate. That's all I still wanted to do, but so much was getting in the way. There was no opportunity to train, and certainly no coach in sight.

I was supposed to have a coach working with me. Ice Capades offered Carlo Fassi a contract to fly in to work with me four times throughout the year. Instead, he chose to do something I have always found peculiar. He sued me. He claimed I owed him for lessons. He had the papers delivered to New York so that I would learn of his betrayal on my opening night at Madison Square Garden. He would have made far more by taking the contract with Ice Capades to work with me. The lawsuit made no sense because my parents had never received an unpaid bill from him. In fact, my father had a letter from Carlo, dated sometime in 1971, stating that if I came to Colorado and left the Dunfields, Carlo would teach me for free, yet my parents still insisted on paying him. He would have his students buy their lessons ahead of time, and the skaters would be given tickets. They would give him a ticket at the beginning of each lesson. Carlo never required me to have a ticket. I wish he had come to me first. If he really thought he was owed money, he could have billed me directly and I would have given him anything he asked for. I would never stiff a coach who took me to the Olympics, no matter what my mother thought of him. My parents and I wanted to fight the lawsuit based on principle, but Ice Capades didn't want any unfavorable press, so they settled the suit.

That fall, I did my first TV special. My guest stars were Gene Kelly and Jim McKay. What a delight to work with both of those wonderful, legendary gentlemen, each so talented in his own respective field. We rehearsed in Los Angeles and taped the show in Toronto. I realized I was loving my time spent in Los Angeles, I'm sure because of Dean, and soon I got my own apartment in Westwood near the campus of UCLA on Kelton Avenue, only a couple blocks from the Viscontis.

Dean was busy touring the tennis circuit,

but he had been flying into as many cities as he could to see me in the show. However, where I liked seeing him best was on his own turf, back in his hometown. I'd watch him play tennis in tournaments in Beverly Hills or Calabasas. He was also taking acting lessons when he could, and going out on auditions. He soon realized that he had to distinguish his name from his famous father's. He decided he wanted to be called Dean Paul professionally. But to me he was always Dean.

Mom was still not accepting Dean. She continued to make assumptions about him without knowing him because she thought everyone in Hollywood was on drugs and worried I might become involved too. It goes to show how little she understood me. She must have said something to Jerry Weintraub. One time in his office, he looked straight at me and said seriously, "Don't get mixed up in this cocaine stuff." He had another high-profile client whose life had been overcome by it, so he was well aware of the dangers. Dean and I were both athletes who were very in tune with our bodies. That was how we made our livings. We knew what we had to do to keep ourselves in shape, and doing drugs never crossed my mind. I don't know about Dean. He certainly never did them while I was with him. But maybe my mom was so paranoid about it because of her own habit of self-medicating. Maybe she worried that her affliction might have passed down to her children. My dad must have felt the same way, but as usual they played good cop, bad cop: My mom verbalized the negative feelings so my father could keep smiling.

The truth about Dean was that he came from one of the most loving families I have ever met. His father, Dean Martin, was kind, warm, welcoming, and dear. He was funny and adorable, just like his son. He was a larger-than-life figure, yet he was very comfortable to be with and lived a simple life of eating in the same restaurants and coming home to his TV set. He was not a Hollywood party type and didn't love being around strangers. He was happiest surrounded by his children. He adored them and was so proud of them all. Although he was divorced from Jeanne, they still made a happy pair, together for every family occasion. Jeanne's wonderful birthday parties for each of their combined seven children brought their entire clan together several times a year. Jeanne made me feel like a family member the instant I met her. She was such a lovely woman. She always hosted a traditional Christmas Eve party for all their friends who didn't have a family to be with on that night.

From the moment Dean and I started dating, the entire Martin family followed Jeanne's lead and treated me like family. Dean and I would go to Las Vegas to watch his father's show. His hotel suite was always near the showroom because Dean Sr. had an elevator phobia. He watched me on TV and called me "Sassyface" because of my Clairol commercials. His youngest daughter, Gina, had been a skater and wanted to skate in Ice Capades. Juanita gave her private lessons and convinced her to try out. Gina made the chorus line the second year I was in the show. Dean Martin and Dean traveled to see their women skate on opening night in Pittsburgh, 1977. I had such fun touring with Gina.

Dean and I felt comfortable in each other's lives. Because of his own upbringing in the spotlight, fame didn't faze him. It wasn't new to him in the least, and he took it in stride. He also helped me to deal with it, since it was so new and strange to me. He would think it was quite natural that sometimes I had to leave the backstage area between shows wearing a blond wig so I could get a short break.

He also understood why I felt overwhelmed at the press conferences I was expected to hold in each city. I never knew what to say beyond what a nice city I was in and felt awkward talking about myself. For me, it was torture. Luckily, the woman in charge of publicity for Ice Capades, Melanie Wyler, was a very smart lady who saw how uncomfortable I was doing press. She found out about the skating clinics I was teaching in my free time. The classes were very special to me. They were for blind children.

In the early '70s, I had met a blind skater in Wilmington, Delaware, by the name of Stash Serafin, when I skated in a show for Ron Ludington's rink. I was moved to tears by Stash's courageous performance: He didn't let his blindness stop him from expressing his passion on the ice. Of course, I wanted to know how he didn't run into the boards. Stash told me he could tell by the sound of his blade on the ice if he was getting close to the boards. He also could feel the warmth of the spotlight on him and how it changed when he was nearer the side of the rink. I was inspired by Stash and I remember my mother telling me, "Someday you could teach kids like that." That planted a seed in my head.

Post-Olympics, I had begun teaching a skating class for children who came on a bus to Culver City Rink from the Los Angeles

School for the Blind. It was an opportunity for these children to get out and do something completely different, and it was extremely rewarding for me. My goal was to give these kids the same feeling I had when I skated. There was one girl who had braces on her legs and couldn't stand up. So I picked her up and put her on my back. Her little face was right in my ear, and she lit up, filled with the magic of movement.

"Oh, I feel the wind in my face."

The way she said it is something I will never forget. She touched my heart forever.

Melanie suggested the interviewers come to the rink to watch me skate with my friends instead of putting me at a lecturn and trying to make me talk. Together, she and I were able to spread this skating program to other cities through the March of Dimes' participation. Soon I invited other cast members to come in and help to teach, as in each city there would be busloads of kids ready to have a lesson. When we were playing Washington, DC, Eunice Shriver involved us in the Special Olympics.

There was so much to balance in those years. Most of all, I was trying to find balance in my relationship with Dean. He loved to watch me skate and I loved to watch him play tennis. We'd go down to La Costa so that he could train with Pancho Segura. Dean had grown up with Jimmy Connors practicing on the Martins' court. Pancho knew that and said to Dean, "If you worked half as hard as Jimmy, you could be the best." At the end of my first year in Ice Capades, he played in the Queen's Cup at Wimbledon, a qualifier for the Wimbledon Cup. He played with the greatest in the game, including Jimmy Connors, Bjorn Borg, and Vitas Gerulaitis. But he knew he couldn't keep up the pace of traveling and training forever. He had other interests. The thing that held him back was that he was so good at everything he tried.

He had already enjoyed success in the music world when his band, Dino, Desi & Billy, became a sensation in the 1960s and topped the music charts. The band never truly disbanded because Dino, Desi, and Billy were the best of friends. But Dean had other interests he pursued. He was a car racer. He did it under an assumed name because he didn't want his mother to find out. What he really wanted to do was to be a good actor. Robert De Niro was his biggest role model. He had an agent, Charles Roven, who sent him out on many auditions.

It seemed the main thing standing in the way of his blossoming acting career was that he was Dean Martin's son. He wasn't taken seriously when he went in to audition. Too many times he was told he was too good-looking for the part. To him, this was never a compliment, but a stab in the heart of his ambitions. He often said to me, "I want to make a difference in this world." It never occurred to me to think about whether people would remember me after I died, but Dean wanted to leave his mark. Maybe because of his father. He knew his father would leave a legacy behind, and Dean thought he had to live up to what his father represented. There was an unsettledness about Dean. He kept a lot of his true feelings inside, another thing we had in common, and something his dad was also known for doing. I realized all this about Dean early on, but it didn't stop me from falling in love with him. And staying in love. And I knew Dean was in love with me.

He was there for me when, in the fall of my second year in Ice Capades, I was so tired and weak I began to have trouble standing upright. I was about to shoot my third TV special. Since I felt achy and nauseous, I thought I was coming down with the flu. A doctor was brought in to give me a B_{12} shot. He was alarmed by how pale I looked and asked to do a blood test. The test showed that I was anemic and that there was blood in my stool. I was bleeding internally. I was immediately admitted into Cedars-Sinai Medical Center. My TV special was postponed. More testing revealed that I had a bleeding ulcer, but it was impossible to tell how long I'd had it: It could have been there a long time. As a kid, I used to double up in stomach pain, or if I had fruit on an empty stomach, it would burn. My stomach problems had always been attributed to what I was eating. One time I ate a whole can of black olives and became horribly sick. I used to throw up before I skated at competitions — I was so nervous. It didn't matter what I ate before a competition, I managed to throw it up. Even if I didn't eat anything, I would have the same reaction. Competition always felt like I was going to my own execution. I never felt well at competitions. In fact, sometimes I could barely function. That's why I trained so hard. That's why at every session I tried to be the first skater on the ice and the last skater off. I always said to myself, "One more time." It was to avoid the feeling of being unprepared. But it didn't seem to help. I'd get sick anyway, get weak, and start to shake.

Salvation had come in the form of a protein drink recommended by Doris Fleming. She'd said she used to give it to Peggy right before she skated. It filled me up but didn't weigh me down. Once I started with those drinks, I stopped throwing up.

Fortunately, there was a new treatment when my ulcer was discovered that I quickly responded to. It was called cimetidine, and within two weeks of taking it, I started to feel better. I began to eat very bland food and I was fine. I am so grateful that my illness was detected at this time and that it was taken care of by wonderful professionals. Thankfully, I haven't had a problem with my stomach since. But I am very aware of the pain I felt for so many years and am very careful of medications that could potentially cause problems again.

Most of all, it was Dean who helped me through this difficult time. His good-natured spirit was easy and relaxing to be around. He knew my life was a fishbowl, and he not only knew how to handle it, he knew how to help me handle it. I went back on the road and joined the show in Oakland. Dean met me there for Thanksgiving. The only place to get turkey was the hotel coffee shop. We sat in there and had the most memorable Thanksgiving. It was always a breath of fresh air when he came to see me on the road. And everyone else adored him. He had such a great sense of humor. He didn't take things too seriously; he made them nice and always pleasant. We laughed a lot. I wanted us to be together all the time. I wondered if that would ever come true or if it was just a dream.

Long Island Sound,
1961. Me, Sandy,
and Marcia
"ON THE ROCKS"

Mom

My first "Dorothy Hamill"
haircut

The house I grew up in and occasionally slept in

My maternal grandparents, Jonsie and Bill, on the porch of their summer cottage

My first teacher, Barbara Taplin, and me at nine years old

Holding the largest trophy I ever won

July 1968. Ann Gramm presents me with the first-place medal in the Lake Placid Open Free Skate Competition. Notice my pierced ears.

Hula dancing with Valerie Levine. If Arthur Wirtz could have seen me . . .

Gifts from Japanese fans, 1971. Grandpa holds my pearls from the Crown Prince.

*In the Lake Placid Lussi rink
with Carol Vaughn and Jean Fortune*

*Dad helps me
pack for the 1973
Worlds, held in
Czechoslovakia.*

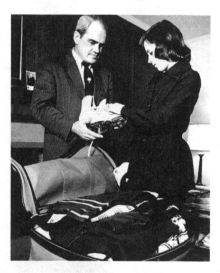

*1974. Flying to
Munich Worlds
with Mom and
Dad. All I have left
of my radix pins is
this photo.*

I catch my breath as Carlo Fassi figures out my next move.

The 1975 United States World Figure Skating Team. Gordie McKellan is to my right. All our games of add-on paid off.

Peter Burroughs comes to my rescue right before the Olympics.

Me receiving my Olympic gold medal, February 13, 1976

John Curry and me playing around before we compete in the '76 Olympics, at the outdoor rink in Garmisch

Backstage during my first year in Ice Capades with two of "Dorothy's Boys," Ricky Swenson and Dean Bates

Part of my Ice Capades family, Papa Smurf and Smurfette

Before makeup, on a three-show Saturday in Chicago, Spring, 1978

It might have been as painful for the audience to listen to me as it was for me to speak.

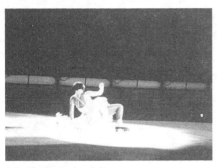

I fell and could not get up.

Deborah Amelon, my friend and coconspirator, in Ice Follies

Just how many of "Dorothy's Boys" does it take to lift me?

Maybe I should have said yes to the hula number after all.

Celebrating my brother's graduation from Yale, with his future wife, "Perky," in 1973

A fan sends me a photo of his collage.

Proud Mom and Dad on Sandy's wedding day

My first Hollywood party. The 1976 Emmys with Jerry and Jane Weintraub, Karen and Richard Carpenter, and John Denver.

Marcia and me at my bridesmaid's luncheon before my wedding to Dean Paul

Our first dance as husband and wife

Suga and me

My two Romeos on and off the ice, enjoying my father-in-law's show in Vegas. How lucky can a girl get!

The Martin family dinner table around Christmas, 1976. Dean, Gina, Ricci, Jeanne, me, and Grandma Peggy.

Showing off the pearls Dean replaced

Hanging out with Dean's dad in London

The picture I hold of Dean in my heart forever. I keep this in my bedroom.

Gus Lussi and Dick Button with me at the Lake Placid Winter Carnival

Proud to work with the two finest men in show business, George Eby and Richard Dwyer

The thrill of a lifetime

Peggy's mom, Doris Fleming, visiting backstage. Universal Amphitheater, 1986.

Giving one of my special little friends a piggyback ride on the ice, feeling the wind on our faces

Another special friend takes to the ice with me.

Serenaded by Gene Kelly in my first TV special

Best buddy and cookie smuggler Kathy Porter, at my home in Benedict Canyon

Sonja and Peter Dunfield

Happy Days with Ken on the dance floor

Ken and me with Ben Tisdale. My smile hides my pregnancy nausea.

Alex, at eleven days old

Dad plays the piano as he leads
his orchestra during the late '40s.

Dad sharing his
passion for music
with his grand-
daughter, Alex

Ken and me in
Hong Kong with
our children,
Alex, Jennifer,
and Daniel, just
after we bought
Ice Capades

Alex, at six years
old, grows into
her skates from
Harlick.

Champions on Ice backstage, Mother's Day, 2000, with the Amelons, Dr. Maynard, Jessie, Debbie (in back), Peggy, and Debbie's two sons, Addison and Walker Huddy. Jessie saved my young birthday guests in 1966.

Backstage with Michelle Kwan and Peggy Fleming

Tim Murphy and Nathan Birch, brilliant choreographers and my dearest friends

7
THE HIGH PRICE OF GOLD

No doubt my stomach problems had begun when I was a young girl and were prompted by the stress of competition. But they were also exacerbated by the stresses of growing up in my family home. It was no mystery that these ailments began to clear up once I was away from my parents and out of our Riverside house. Mom and Dad must have been feeling the same way, because they said they were looking to move from there. They said they had to have more privacy. Strangers kept dropping by hoping to meet me. And they were tired of the tabloid news reporters popping in, wanting a story about Dean and me. Sometimes, it became frightening for them. One day, they came home to find a young man sleeping in their garage. He said he was waiting for them and had come to save me. Instead of calling the police about this troubled person, they felt sorry for him. My mom said he looked like he was starving, so she invited him in and fed him. It was Mother's Day and she made him call his mother. Then they took him to the nearest hotel, where his father picked him up. Clearly, this young man showing up and all the other intrusions were my fault. So when Mom asked me to help them buy a new house, I didn't balk. Mom and Dad found a beautiful new home in Cos Cob, just a couple of miles from my childhood home, but a step up in my parents' eyes. My mom had always talked about wanting to live in a nicer part of town, and I finally made it possible for her. They kept our house on Riverside Avenue and rented it out. I continued to pay my parents' bills and kept them on a monthly salary. It occurred to me that they didn't need the money. They had no dependent children. No skating bills. No college bills. My father still worked and they had rental income. But if they were taking the money, I figured I must owe it to them.

My brother and sister were very grateful. For a wedding present I took Sandy, his new wife, and my parents on a cruise to the Greek Islands. It was a rare time with almost all our family together. I also gave Sandy a down payment to buy his first house. I bought Marcia a car a few years later. They didn't ask for these things. I gave them willingly and with love. My parents were different. They *expected* it. I was made to feel very guilty for how the demands of skating had overpowered their lives. How did I make up for all the years they spent sacrificing for me? My guilt and my checkbook were intertwined. Dean and Juanita were both aghast that I was still paying them, but it was difficult to explain to others, even those closest to me, why I felt an obligation to keep it up. I wanted Mom to be happy and have her own money so she wouldn't have to go begging to Dad. It was very important to me, because I knew she felt demeaned that she didn't have her own resources. She was a very independent woman who lived dependent on a man because she had raised a family in a time period when women were discouraged from making their own way. She had earned a wage before she had married my father and before she'd had children. Who knows what she could have become in the working world if she hadn't had to manage my skating career? She was very strong and smart. I honestly felt that my gestures and gifts would help make her happy.

I also wanted her to be happy about my relationship with Dean. We had hardly spoken in the year since our fight over him. It was February 1978 and Marcia was about to get married. Marcia doubted whether Mom wanted Dean at the wedding, but with Marcia's permission, I brought him. I was deeply in love with him, and it was important to me that my parents realized it. When he walked in to meet everyone, there were audible gasps. The gasps were not only because I had brought him but also because he was so incredibly handsome. He had that effect on people. He proceeded to charm everyone. He paid special attention to my mother. It took more than a normal dose of his charm to get her to melt, but eventually she warmed up to him.

There was nothing *not* to like about Dean. When he and my mother had first met two summers earlier at the Beverly Hills Hotel, he had taken her hand and said, "Nice to meet you, Carol." I was horrified. We were raised to call the parents of our friends by their surnames only. Immediately, my mother sensed the differences in our backgrounds. But Dean was able to laugh about it and make us forget the differences. At that time, Mom disapproved of Dean because it didn't seem he ever had a real job. But now he did. Dean was about to star opposite Ali MacGraw in *Players*. It was a major Paramount movie, and it was being filmed in Mexico and London. Robert Evans, the for-

mer head of Paramount, who had shep-
herded films like *Love Story, The Godfather,*
and *Chinatown,* was producing it. It was
written by one of the most prominent writers in Hollywood, Arnold Schulman, whose
credits included *Funny Lady* and *Goodbye,
Columbus.* The movie role was a chance of a
lifetime for Dean and we all knew it. But he
contracted hepatitis while working in Mexico and nearly died. He was sick in the hospital for weeks. It was a struggle for him to
finish the part. He spent months recuperat-
ing at his mother's house afterward. It took a
whole year before he felt almost normal.

Earlier in the shoot, I had gone to England
to watch him film on the court at Wimbledon. But Dean's behavior was very strange
toward me. He was suddenly very cold and
never invited me to the set. He didn't seem
to want me there. I felt so unwelcome; I left
London with suspicions something was
going on that I did not know about. I had
absolutely no proof, it was just a feeling I
had. The problem was, we were each so busy
in our lives we were rarely in the same town.
I never found out if he had been unfaithful
to me at this time. There was no way I knew
how to get such an answer from him. All I
knew was that I was staying faithful to him.
Luckily, the constant of my life was skating,

and as always, it was keeping me afloat, above my worries.

At the end of 1979, I did a TV special that lifted my spirits. It was set in Lake Placid and shot in time to be aired for the 1980 Olympics. The theme was "going home" and it was titled *My Corner of the Sky*: It was about the part of my childhood spent in Lake Placid, but it was also a promotion for the Lake Placid Olympics. The skating sequences were done outdoors on the many lakes and rivers around our cozy Adirondack town. The last day of the shoot, we were on the frozen Cascade River that flowed next to the road leading into town. That day, there was a blizzard that settled into gusting winds. Everyone else stayed in the truck while I did my routine around the reeds growing through the ice. I was by myself out on the ice with my music cueing me in my ear. As I did my Wally jumps down the ice, a gust of wind caught me and floated me into the air. I had never felt anything like it. The crew kept encouraging me to get out of the cold and I had some notion it was freezing, but I was enjoying myself too much. I did it again and again to get the sensation of floating higher and jumping farther than I ever had. Earlier, my stand-in, Peggy Sue Amelon, performed my number for the cameramen to mark the jumps and spins. She measured double for the Wally jumps, just in case, because she knew mine were big. Being carried by the wind, I exceeded the double mark. I felt like I was flying.

Dean joined me in Lake Placid for the Olympics. I rehearsed after all the events were over, late at night, choreographing the number I was going to do in the closing ceremonies accompanied by Chuck Mangione. We were in the audience, on our feet, cheering "U-S-A" with tears in our eyes when the U.S. hockey team beat the USSR. I have witnessed many great Olympic moments, but this was the most thrilling, because I knew too well, from my own competition years, what it meant to beat the Soviet Union. Now the United States had managed to beat a whole team of USSR athletes who had been playing together for years. They were professional, subsidized by their government and heroes in their country. Our team members were unknown amateurs who had just met and joined forces a few months earlier. As the crowd was hailing the American victory, Dean proudly turned to me.

"You know, you did that once."

Not until this moment, and not until Dean said this, did I fully realize the magnitude of winning an Olympic gold medal and what it meant. When I won, I was in another country where another language was spoken. So it felt like what John Curry said when he won his gold the same year: "This is just a step along the way." It felt like just one more notch on the belt, one more competition to win. I didn't realize until this moment what a great pinnacle of achievement it was in the eyes of the world, especially when an athlete was up against the extraordinary talent of the Eastern bloc countries.

Soon after that, I bought a house in the Pacific Palisades section of Los Angeles. It was a lovely Cape Cod, a style that made me feel I was back East, and it was right on Sunset Boulevard. I began decorating the home to make it feel more like mine. That summer, Dean and Juanita planned a birthday party for me at my new home. Juanita gave Dean the job of getting some of the food. He had to admit he had never been inside a grocery store, an indication of his upbringing with housekeepers and cooks catering to him. He laughed and said to give him another job he could handle, like going to Vendome for the liquor. I insisted on baking my own cake, because I loved to bake. Baking always brought back warm memories for me, first of my grandmother and me during summers in Rockport, then continuing the tradition when my mom and I lived in Colorado. It felt heavenly to be baking in my own kitchen in my first home.

My mom sent me a present and I opened it at the party. It was my recipe album from 1973, a collection of recipes in my own handwriting. They were from our years spent together in Colorado, when cooking was the only thing that bonded us unconditionally and without criticism. There was the recipe for Guacamole, Carrot Cake, Coconut Chicken, Red Velvet Cake, French Onion Soup, Pumpkin Ice Cream Pie, and, of course, the Granola Date Coffee Cake recipe I'd found on the side of the cereal box.

I didn't show tenderness at receiving this gift. I didn't break down and forgive my mother for all her negative judgment. My reaction revealed the mind-set I had at that time toward her. Although I later thanked her, at this party I didn't say, "What a great gift!" Instead, I followed Juanita's lead and *laughed* at it. Juanita took it from me and jostled it around, making it seem like nothing. She expected something extravagant from my parents: Her standard of acceptability would be something from Gucci or Van Cleef & Arpels. She said that for all the money I was sending my parents, they could have bought me a decent gift. Instead, my mother had sent me something that was already mine. I was too ignorant to see that she was sending me something far more precious than money could buy. She sent me one of the most cherished possessions I have today. But it was impossible to understand that because my parents were making our relationship all about material "things." Also, I didn't see that Juanita knew she couldn't compete with a recipe box for my attention so, of course, she would denigrate it. I was just beginning to grow up. I was a late bloomer. I had been focused on a goal for so long that I hadn't learned about feelings and relationships.

I felt good about paying my parents back, but it seemed they were still expecting more. They had no idea how much of my earnings were already disappearing to managers, press agents, and Uncle Sam. And they really had no idea how hard I was working: It was much harder, and in a different way, from the Olympics. They couldn't understand that the grinding physical repetition of so many performances was exhausting. Life on the road was tough, and I never really got used to it. My body was trained to go to sleep at nine and get up before dawn. Now it was nearly the opposite. We didn't get back to the hotel until midnight and then it took time to wind down. We wouldn't be in bed until early morning. I usually had to rise early and look good for a TV show — *Good Morning, Wherever We Were*. It was impossible to get a good night's sleep. The hotels were always full of revelers late at night or tourist groups making noise early in the morning. The hotel staff would often tell the curiosity-seekers which room I was in, and they would knock on the door, waking me up. If it wasn't them knocking, it was the housekeepers, who had no clue that we had been up all night. One time, when Dean came on the road to visit me, we had a rare Sunday morning to sleep in together. I had done three shows the day before and wanted to rest up for the two shows always scheduled on Sundays. A housekeeper kept knocking on our door, even though I had the "Do Not Disturb" sign on the knob. She would not go away after both Dean and I asked her to. She was knocking on everyone's doors, shouting, "Let me into your room! I have to finish my cleaning and go home!" It was about eleven in the morning, which is sunrise to show people.

Finally, I lost my temper. I got out of bed and opened the door. Facing her, I shouted, "We don't get to go home. This is our home.

This is where we sleep. This is the only sanctuary we have. Please don't disturb us. Don't knock on the door when you see this sign!" I must have been quite the sight. "America's Sweetheart" standing in the hallway in her pj's giving hell to a hotel housekeeper.

Suddenly, I heard cheering from down the hallway. Other skaters had heard my rant, stepped outside their rooms, and were applauding my bravery. I guess it was something the show people had wanted to say for years. It was true that these hotel rooms were the only sanctuary we had. We traveled with items to try and make our temporary living spaces homey. I remember one skater who would open her trunk to reveal photographs from home, as if they were on her own dresser. Another would burn incense. But our paltry attempts were always short-lived. I had a cassette player and a beautiful robe from Dean that were stolen a year later. They were stolen from the same hotel where I shouted at the housekeeper.

Some of the skaters carried a hot pot with them because it was so difficult to find restaurants that were open when we weren't performing. I soon bought one, and started existing on ramen noodles and canned soup. The hotel restaurants, if there were any, wouldn't open until after we'd left for the show and they'd be closed when we got back. No one had a car, so we couldn't go anywhere. We were at the mercy of whatever there was near the hotel. But usually there was nothing and no place to walk to. Our hotels were near the arenas, where there was little else but warehouses and industrial parks. Skaters would stuff themselves with food on Saturday, when the show would feed us at a buffet, but there was nothing on Sunday. In each succeeding year, I began to explore other places to stay and started to treat myself to finer hotels. But it came at a price, and I don't mean the bill at the end of the week.

Since I was away from the other show people, it made me feel more isolated on the road. My friend Kim Danks had left to go back to school and been replaced by a professional assistant who could handle all my fan mail and other details of business. Her name was Katherine McVeigh and she was wonderful to be around, but it wasn't the same as having an old friend to pal with. We both tried desperately to find a normal existence. Juanita came from time to time, but she was beginning to turn people off. Once, in Cincinnati, she caused a scene with my fellow cast member and friend, Kathy Porter. Kathy had brought me some cookies from an after-party and left them in front of my door. They were the kind of peanut-butter cookies that Kathy knew I loved. It was a fun gesture on her part to think of me. But Juanita must have been watching my door like a hawk because she caught Kathy and screamed at her, "Don't sneak food to her! I'm supposed to be watching what she eats!" Juanita saw Kathy as some kind of threat. It was as if I gained an ounce, Juanita would lose her job. Juanita wanted to control me, and kept the other skaters at a distance. I was starting to grow up and realized that I didn't need someone to control me, that I was doing okay on my own. Instead of helping me to assimilate into the show lifestyle, she was now standing in the way. She had helped me with my weight in the beginning and had been my sounding board for many years. I was grateful to her, but this episode with the cookies was over the top and I knew it. For us, it was the beginning of the end. I was no longer dependent on her for approval of my relationship with Dean. My mom, however, was starting to show her approval.

It was a wonder Mom was able to show feelings for anything else or anybody else at that point, because it was discovered that she had breast cancer. Marcia told me, not Mom.

"Did Mom tell you?" Marcia asked me.

"Tell me what?"

"She spotted some redness on her breast but didn't go in to the doctor right away. When she did, a biopsy was performed and it was malignant."

I was dumbstruck. My own mother had cancer, and I'd had to find out from my sister.

I rushed home in between Ice Capades dates. Mom had a mastectomy so extensive surgeons had to take out some of her lymph nodes. At that time, survival rates were so low, the diagnosis of breast cancer was a death sentence. She would have to go on chemo for one year.

For the first time in my life, I felt sorry for my mother. She was the strongest and toughest person I knew, and probably will ever know. To see someone so tough be so vulnerable was a wake-up call to me. I realized not only how precious life is, but also how precious she was to me. She displayed her characteristic strength throughout the whole ordeal of being on chemotherapy. She never said, "Why me?" She never complained: She accepted everything she had to go through to try and get well. I went home as often as I could during this time and kept positive thoughts all throughout. I never let myself think that we were going to lose her: I never wanted to think it might happen. I wanted so much to help her, but it was her strength that sustained us all. She was matter-of-fact about her hair falling out and how the doctor had told her to keep an ice cap on her head to help save her hair. When it fell out anyway and she broke out in sweats she still did not complain. Mom never lost her sense of humor throughout: She used it as a tool to help her through it. I can't tell you how many nights Marcia and I agonized over her situation. We both admired our mother's strength and we were so inspired at her will to carry on. We realized that she'd always had vulnerabilities, but we'd never seen them growing up because she never wanted us to see them. She'd allowed me to stay immersed in my self-centered world, in order to succeed. I know it was my mother's strength that enabled her to survive: The same strength she always showed that helped make me a champion also made her a champion winning against the odds. Our entire family worried, thinking we might lose her. She was the glue in our family. I thank God that she made it. She became a proud cancer survivor.

The experience helped me learn more about my mother. I began to understand why she wasn't able to come to the Olympic Arena to enjoy my victory. That day was tough on her. She was seeing the end of her own life as she knew it, and once the goal was achieved, she had to take a hard look at herself. The goal may have been the temporary glue that kept my parents' marriage together. Thankfully, my parents did stay together, and it became clear that my skating wasn't temporary glue. But she had no way of knowing that at the time. After I turned professional, my parents became closer. They had less stress, and more time to be together and enjoy themselves. The two of them could make each other laugh like no other couple I knew.

Now able to enjoy her husband, my mom wanted me to have a good relationship with a man. She wanted me to have a happy marriage and have children. Dean and I had been dating for six years and I hoped one day our relationship might lead to marriage. But, for now, I was very happy and having fun being his girlfriend. Almost losing my mother to cancer made the people I loved even more precious to me. It was 1981. I must have been acting more seriously toward Dean because one day, out of the blue, he completely shocked me by proposing. He didn't ask me to marry him in the textbook, old-fashioned sense: He didn't get down on one knee and say, "Will you marry me?" Instead, he presented me with a little black box and sweetly said, "Open it." I opened it and in it was a beautiful ring, a gold band simply adorned with four baguette diamonds.

With my jaw dropping in surprise, he asked, "Do you know what that is?"

I looked up at him and shrugged my shoulders. Beyond it being a beautiful ring, I had no idea what he meant.

"It's an engagement ring," he said.

"Really?" I asked.

He nodded.

I think I knew in my heart that he wasn't ready to take that step again. So this really came as a complete shock to me. I never expected a proposal. I always harbored the fantasy of one day having a *Leave It to Beaver* life with a picket fence and wonderful children. But Dean and I never once talked about getting married. Yet, I didn't hesitate. I was completely in love with him.

"Yes!" I hugged him.

Then came the hard part.

He said, "Pick a date." Finding five days out of our busy schedules was nearly impossible. When *Players* didn't do as well as expected at the box office and the acting offers didn't flow into his agent's office, he began to take his love of flying to the next level. He had attained the rank of second lieutenant after graduating from officer candidates' school, which would lead to pilot training all over the country. He knew he'd be gone for a long time, and he didn't want me to end up with someone else. I think that's why he wanted to get married. We finally found a date, January 8, 1982. We both knew we wanted the wedding to be in Los Angeles. It was now my home too.

Mom finished her chemotherapy treatments and was happy her hair was growing back. I didn't want to put additional stress on her so I told her Jeanne would help me plan the wedding. Jeanne knew just what to do. She knew all the places and knew how to plan parties. Mom still wanted to help, so she took charge of the out-of-town guests as the time grew near. She now totally accepted Dean. The engagement had made all the difference. Meanwhile, Dean's main concern was that I sell my Palisades house, because he wanted to feel that we were starting out together. I loved that idea, and we had fun house-hunting. He wanted to be closer to where he grew up, so we bought a house in the Benedict Canyon section of Beverly Hills.

The wedding plans had to take place long-distance, because of my commitment to Ice Capades, professional competitions, and my new project, *The Nutcracker.* Working on *The Nutcracker* opened my eyes to the thrill of performing in the theater setting. It prepared me for the next fabulous opportunity that came my way. John Curry, my friend from our Colorado days and the men's Olympic champion the same year I won, invited me to be a part of his new company of skaters. Known as the "Nureyev of the Ice," John was held in the highest regard by the world's most elite skaters because he was a pioneer both on and off the ice. Totally devoted to the art of skating, he was first to combine ballet and modern dance with figure skating. He had turned down lucrative offers from commercial ice shows to form his own company. His idea was to perform in theaters instead of large arenas. He had performed with his company of skaters at the Royal Albert Hall in London. I was honored that he asked me to join and proud to know John well. He had come out publicly as a gay man right before the 1976 Olympics. It could have ruined his chances of winning, but it was important to him to be honest and never pretend to be something he wasn't. Janet Lynn had also been asked to join, and it was seen as her comeback after she left Ice Follies due to health problems. John had overcome so much in his own life. His father never approved of his skating and only came to see him skate twice. When he was sixteen, he had moved to London to work and pay for his own lessons. John was known for being an artist and I was known for being an athlete. Even though I was gaining a new appreciation of the beauty inherent in our sport, I had so much to learn. Skating with his company, I learned there was so much more to skating than jumping and spinning. I felt that John had opened my eyes and my soul to help me discover the artist buried deep within me. I saw skating in a whole new light.

I was so happy to finally be learning from John. I hadn't been able to fully grasp his genius during the years we were together in Denver. First of all, I had found my niche as an athletic skater and there hadn't been any hours in the day left — between school, patch sessions, ballet class, free skating, and homework — to learn anything else. Secondly, John and the rest of us skaters had rarely been at the Denver rink at the same time. He was older, so he hadn't had to worry about school and homework. While we'd been stuck at desks, he had the rink to himself. He'd be leaving just as we would arrive. Little did I know how much I had missed. Now I had the luxury of taking hours of classes with John Curry. It was exhilarating. The ugly duckling inside of me was trying to become a swan — as I always had pictured Peggy Fleming and Janet Lynn.

Dean was very supportive of my need to work with John Curry. He understood my frustration. I wasn't an artist and I wanted to become one. I wanted to improve my skating and become a complete performer. I could only do this if I worked with John Curry. When Dean met John, the two of them hit it off in a way so unexpected, it both surprised and delighted me. On the surface they seemed like polar opposites: The Hollywood insider who had sought and found early commercial success versus the visionary dancer who had sought and found artistic freedom. They were both shy out of their element, but had a mutual respect for each other: They were creative men who appreciated each other's originality.

Unfortunately, my new manager had little appreciation of John Curry's work and would have been happier if I was doing the hula. I had to find a new manager after Jerry Weintraub decided to become a full-time movie producer and stopped managing clients. Juanita had convinced me I should go with Michael Rosenberg. Michael wasn't a manager. I was his first and only client for several years. He didn't like the low-pay offer from the John Curry Skating Company. I tried to explain that it wasn't about the money. Sometimes Michael made me feel like his racehorse, and he didn't want me to waste time on anything that wasn't lucrative for him. He didn't understand my need to grow. He insisted that all I needed to do was go out on the ice, smile, and do that "blur" spin. I still had to earn money with my skating, so I continued to fulfill my other obligations, but the times I spent in John Curry's company sustained me in the difficult years to come. They were years that were to be fraught with unimaginable obstacles.

8
LOVE ON THE RUN

My fairy-tale wedding began at the All Saints Episcopal Church in Beverly Hills. My dad was a devout Episcopalian, and he had raised his family in the faith. The reception was at the Bel-Air Country Club, with two hundred guests, including my family and friends, and Martin family friends like Frank and Barbara Sinatra, and Kirk Kerkorian. It was Dean's idea to wear his lieutenant's dress uniform and he proudly did so. We honeymooned at the Pointe Resort in Phoenix. It was close and easy to get to. We could only stay three days, because we each had to go our separate ways, he to fly F-4 Phantoms and me to entertain.

Summers were traditionally slow for me, as far as touring on the road. I relished staying home with Dean and making his favorite breakfast every morning — eggs, bacon, sourdough toast, freshly squeezed orange juice, chocolate milk, and hot tea. I enjoyed our life and things seemed happy and right. We spent time on his uncle's boat down in Laguna. I loved to be with Dean's son, Alex, who was a beautiful child in every way. Alex was a perfect combination of his handsome father and stunning mother, the actress Olivia Hussey. He was shy and sweet, with a wonderfully silly sense of humor. It was delightful to witness Dean being a dad and experience the special bond they had. Sometimes I felt sad for them. I know Dean felt a sense of guilt for not being able to spend more time with Alex. I never wanted Alex to feel he had to share his time with his dad, so he knew he was welcome at our house anytime. He liked staying with us and loved my chocolate chip cookies, claiming they were the best he'd ever tasted.

There was a part of Dean's personality that no one could touch, not even his own son. Dean wasn't capable of giving himself completely to any person. He always said to me he needed to make something of himself, like his father had. With the early success of Dino, Desi & Billy, he had made a great deal of money. But by the time I met him, he had spent most of it. He told stories about some of the wild things he'd purchased. He had bought a tank and reveled in driving it down Beverly Drive in Beverly Hills. There were also racecars and helicopters. All of that was in his life before we met.

Dean would not have chosen to be a Hollywood playboy living off his family's money even if he could have. He needed and desperately wanted to work. The Martins didn't believe in giving their children an easy ride, as they had seen so many other Hollywood families do. Instead, they wanted to give each of their children the incentive to work. Dean was struggling to get an acting job. He was taking acting lessons and getting to know great actors. James Woods became a mentor and a friend to him. Dean worked weekends out at March Air Force Base in Riverside as an Air National Guard Reserve pilot, and he had wonderful buddies out there. He worked hard at everything he did, but I saw a stronger sense of determination about getting into the Air Force than I had seen in him before. A college degree was mandatory.

He went back to USC to finish his degree so that he would be eligible. He had played football at USC before I met him. He described himself as a "very wide receiver," to avoid getting tackled. When I saw photos of him from this era, I was amazed to see a bulked-up Dean, with such a thick neck and long hair I barely recognized him. He said his mother had burst into tears one evening at the dinner table, as he piled on the food to stay hefty, exclaiming, "I hate what you've done to your body!" He got sidetracked out of USC when he was drafted to play semi-pro in Las Vegas. It took the Air Force to get him to go back and finish. Then he flew to the Pentagon to talk to a general about an age waiver, since he was six months too old for the program. It seemed like nothing was going to stop him. Yet he didn't want to make it his full-time profession. He felt anxious if we took a day or two just to be together because it meant time away from the acting career he was trying so hard to make a success. The one career where he easily would have found instant success was singing. He had innate talent.

Dean had the most beautiful singing voice! But he only saw it as his hobby. His own father didn't believe he was a good singer himself, so their humble opinion of their voices must have run in the family. Dean loved music and had been the lead singer of Dino, Desi & Billy when he was a teenager. But as an adult, he'd never considered it seriously as a career. I remember when he was asked to sing in an Ann-Margret television special. He sang a song originally performed by Melissa Manchester entitled "Come In from the Rain," which showed his amazing range. While he practiced for the taping, he would sing it so beautifully around the house that it would bring me to tears.

The song is about reaching one's potential, and he might as well have been singing about himself, because he was trying so hard to find satisfaction in what he believed was his true calling as an actor. At the taping, everyone was astounded at his ability to sing with genuine heart and soul. I secretly wished he would pursue his singing. Today I understand that, as much as he loved music and singing, he didn't want to have that kind of lifestyle again — he had been through it. He was starting anew with acting. But the Hollywood community wasn't taking him seriously because of his famous pedigree and because they assumed he wasn't taking his acting career seriously enough, although he had a critically acclaimed part in *Heart Like a Wheel.* He found himself forced to downplay his participation in the Air National Guard Reserve. He loved flying and was compelled to serve his country, and this was how he chose to do it.

It must have been difficult for him to emotionally support both a famous dad and a famous wife, but he did. He came to London while my new numbers were being choreographed, and we were able to see his dad perform at the Royal Albert Hall. Dean Sr. sang more songs and joked less than in his Las Vegas act. He earned rave reviews crooning "Return to Me," "Everybody Loves Somebody Sometime," and "Little Ole Wine Drinker Me." It was impossible to believe that both he and his talented son thought of themselves as mediocre vocalists, but they did. Dean Sr. had a comfort and ease about him when he performed. Even though I never saw Dean perform onstage, I was fortunate to hear him sing often, and he really had a great musical talent.

Dean and I made every effort to be together. I visited him while he was training in Columbus, Mississippi, where I had the chance to fly with him. He and a fellow student were training in the T-37, then the T-38, a version of the F-4 Phantom. They decided to rent a Cessna just for fun, so they could fly me around Mississippi. The two guys were showing me what they did every day. Dean was so happy hanging out with his instructors and fellow students. I could see how they came alive when they were flying. Some of my nicest memories of Dean are from Columbus. He was so happy to be doing something he loved so much. And feeling he was doing something important.

That winter, I was back in Lake Placid for a very happy event — in fact, a milestone for me. It was old-home week, seeing so many people I knew from my childhood, as I was crowned Queen of the 1982 Winter Carnival, and my king was Gustave Lussi. Here I was, sitting alongside my mentor and hero, at a ceremony in the Olympic Arena. Part of me felt I wasn't worthy of this honor just because I'd won a gold medal. Yet, I also relished the sense that Mr. Lussi and I were now peers and had officially bonded on some higher plane. Maybe now I could call him Gus.

I flew from Lake Placid to my next stop, Tokyo, with John Curry's company. Dean had never been to Japan, and he kept us all laughing with his inability to forsake his steak and potatoes sustenance for Japanese fare that he didn't understand. He was always so charming and in awe of all the skaters. They loved his funny take on all things human. On this particular trip with me, he could relax, sleep late, read his scripts, and work out at a leisurely pace. For him, it was worth the long trip overseas because it was a magnificent show. We skated to a two-hundred-piece orchestra inside the Yoyogi Stadium. Before we traveled, the orchestra had sent tapes to us so that we could rehearse to their music. Normally, we would have to adapt our programs when we performed live to an orchestra's music because of the requisite tempo changes. But when we arrived for the show, there was no need to finesse anything, as the orchestra performed exactly as they had on the tapes. It was a testament to the precision of the Japanese.

The location of our show was also a testament to the ingenuity of the Japanese, because we skated on a gigantic indoor swimming pool that had been frozen solely for our performance. The bars for the diving boards were still around its edges. The surface was approximately three times the size of a standard NHL rink, much too large for our timed programs: We had to fight against our skater's natural instincts to cover the entire ice and were forced to stay in the center. It was January 1983 and Japan still didn't have very many ice rinks.

The Japanese were clamoring to see Janet Lynn again after falling in love with her at their 1972 Olympics. I know I wasn't a big hit. John Curry had chosen a beautiful piece of music from a movie entitled *Victory at Sea,* which was all about the battle at Midway — not a good choice for Japan. I don't know how many people in the audience knew that, but I am horrified at the thought that I might have offended the Japanese. John had chosen it because it reminded him of my strong Olympic music by Korngold, especially the selection from *Sea Hawk*. There were so many outstanding skaters in this company, all handpicked by John Curry not for their competitive medal records but for their ability to combine the artistry of dance and skating. One of them was Laurie Nichol, who would go on to become one of the premiere choreographers in our sport by doing programs for Michelle Kwan, Brian Boitano, the Canadian pair team of Jamie Salé and David Pelletier, and the 2006 World Champion, Kimmie Meisner.

Around this time I changed to a new accountant. He called me one day, saying he had noticed how much money was going to my parents each month and he was worried. He said, "You can't keep paying your parents like this." It was a wake-up call to me. I realized I could no longer sustain them, but more importantly, I no longer wanted our ties to be financial. I just wanted a normal parent-child relationship. I suppose that they were thinking that since I was paying 15 percent to a manager and had other professionals on the payroll, they deserved to be paid also. It wasn't that they didn't deserve to be paid. But as a practical matter, it had to come to an end. I tried to talk to them rationally about this issue. They ignored my attempts, switching subjects and refusing to discuss it. It came to the point where I asked my accountant to write a letter to them. It was written on his stationery and stated that I had to look after myself as I was now married and wanted to start a family of my own. I wanted to rein in my expenses and take control of my own finances. I had given this a lot of thought. It was time to grow up and plan for my future. To do this, I had to discontinue paying them month after month.

The response from my father sent me into a tailspin. I heard nothing for weeks, then a long, handwritten letter arrived from my father. He wrote, "You made it in spades and you owe us." He detailed what he and Mom had done for me to get me where I was. He wrote, "How dare you?" to my request that I take them off my payroll. I was devastated. I showed the letter to Dean, my hands shaking. He read it and his eyes got teary, feeling so awful for me. I read that letter over and over again. After the initial shock, the hurt set in. It was so painful and made me so angry that I tore the letter into little bits.

I needed time to sort out what the letter

said and what it meant to us as a family. It wasn't that I wouldn't or couldn't help them financially; it was that I wasn't able to give as much. I wanted the amount to be reasonable. Soon I was back on the road, and when Ice Capades played Washington, DC, I felt ready to call my parents to confront them. It was late and after the show. Mom answered the phone. Dad was asleep in his chair, his usual position after his round of cocktails.

"Mom, how could you send that letter to me?"

"What are you talking about?"

"The letter Dad wrote to me!"

"What do you mean?" she asked innocently.

She pretended that she didn't know anything about it. I had to get past her denial.

"It's not fair what he said to me and you know it!" I exclaimed.

"The letter you sent to us was not very fair, Dorothy." I could tell by the tone of her voice that she had been drinking.

"I'm talking about the letter Dad and you sent to me! It was mean. How could you say those things?"

"What a mean thing to send your parents."

"Mom, I paid your back taxes because I knew I owed you those. You went into debt for my skating but also for Sandy's education. I bought you a house, a car, so much else. I did it because I wanted to and I did it all lovingly. But it has to stop somewhere. The monthly income is too much. I've been paying you and Dad for seven years!"

"I don't know what you are talking about. No, you haven't. You haven't given me anything." That was the lowest blow.

"What? I've been giving you a weekly allowance!"

"I haven't gotten anything."

"I set it up so you would get a weekly allowance!"

"No, you didn't."

Dad had woken up when I'd called, but he was staying quiet.

"Put Dad on."

"Your dad is tired."

"So am I. Let me talk to him."

Dad got on the phone. "This has been very difficult on your mother and me."

"Why is Mom telling me I haven't done anything for her? She says there wasn't a weekly allowance for her!"

"I don't know. Maybe now is not the time to talk about this."

I was insistent. "Dad, tell Mom about the allowance for her."

"You know I am not going to get between the two of you."

He gave the phone back to my mom.

"No, I want you both to get on the phone! Dad, you know having Mom get this allowance was very important to me," I kept on, hoping they were both listening. "I hated that Mom went without. I hated that she had to go begging to you. She never said to me, No, you can't have that. She didn't deny me. By setting up this allowance, I was changing all that. She shouldn't have to go begging to you, Dad. YOU NEVER TOLD HER ABOUT THE ALLOWANCE, DID YOU?"

He was silent. I don't even know if he was on the phone.

"DID YOU!?"

"Dorothy, don't yell at your father!"

"Mom, he still has you going to him for money! You really don't know a portion was to go straight to you every week, do you?

"No, I don't," she answered, confused.

"You let him control everything coming from me, didn't you?"

"He's always handled the finances."

"This was supposed to be for you, Mom! If you wanted to get your hair done, or a present for your grandchildren — or a ticket for a Broadway show. Just for you to decide. Dean called it mad money."

I was crying hysterically. What had I worked for all these years? What had my mother worked for? I wanted her to have the freedom she deserved. She never had a chance to make her own money. For six years I thought I was giving her that chance. This weekly amount was to allow her to spend money that she didn't have to defend to my dad. I had never discussed it with her because I had assumed she was getting the allowance. She'd never discussed it with me because she knew from my dad that they were getting money from me. With all the other things I was paying for — houses, vacations, taxes, cars, and extravagant gifts, like jewelry for my mother — the weekly allowance had been overlooked. But it was the one thing of which I was most proud.

My friend Kathy Porter and two other girlfriends were in my hotel room. They heard the whole thing. Kathy had heard me talking about this allowance for a long time prior to this call, knowing it was something I was proud of.

The ranting and raving went on. My father had been controlling their finances and had never given Mom her share. My mom didn't know who to believe. I didn't know who to believe either. They banded together and ganged up against me. I was their ungrateful daughter.

"You don't love *me*. You just want money

from me," I tearfully insisted.

"You owe it to us, Dorothy," they were telling me. They didn't care about me, they didn't care that I wanted their love with no strings attached — they were only interested in money. To my mom and dad, dollars equaled love. After this phone call, we didn't speak for a year.

I wondered what would have happened if I hadn't won the gold medal. Would my parents still have expected me to support them indefinitely? There were thousands of parents who paid for their children to skate and to compete without ever winning anything; thousands who had gotten up at five in the morning, driven their kids many hundreds of miles, year after year, and agonized over managing the details of a figure skater's life; thousands who had done the same thing my parents had done. Did all these parents expect eternal payback? I don't know. And would my relationship with my parents be better if I had not won? Maybe. But their demands had little to do with money. It went deeper. It would take me years to learn just how deep. Now that I am a parent, I know how I feel. I have given my daughter every opportunity to find something she loves to do. I never expect anything in return other than love and, hopefully, someday, appreciation for doing my best. She will never owe me anything other than respect. Parents are supposed to help their children. They are our responsibility. We bring them into this world. It is our job to help them find their way.

But the situation with my parents was more complicated. They craved recognition from me. They wanted me to realize how much they had done for me and the money became that validation. They certainly didn't need me to get by. My father was still working and bringing in a paycheck. I had paid all their debts. They knew they weren't going to starve without being on my payroll. Then why did they make me feel so guilty?

It was up to me to shed the guilt. I thought I had been very generous to my family and friends, so I started to treat myself to something I loved — jewelry. I began collecting pieces from all over the world. Buying far more than I could ever wear, I built an amazing collection, representing all the places I had been. When I was a competitive skater with no money, I had developed an earnest appreciation for jewelry by earning the treasured Radix pins. These were gold pins in the shape of a skating blade and given by the USFSA to the American medal winners at Nationals, Worlds, and the Olympics. The first-place gold pin had a diamond beautifully positioned in the toepick and was engraved with our title, placement, and category. I had earned nine of these pins and I was very proud of them. And I was proud that now I could buy jewelry for myself. I bought a few unique pieces from Van Cleef & Arpels, and I even bought a beautiful, original piece from my mother-in-law, Jeanne Martin, a piece that Dean Sr. had given her.

My jewelry collection represented more than pretty things to wear: It constituted *all* that was truly mine. I didn't want people to buy it for me because I wanted to feel it was something I had earned. Also, I admit now, the quest for original pieces of expensive jewelry filled the loneliness I felt when I was away from Dean. While working kept me positive and up, I knew I couldn't keep up this kind of lifestyle forever. How was I ever going to have my cozy home with children, where I would bake chocolate chip cookies for my loved ones? As it was, being married to Dean wasn't different from when we were dating. It was still love on the run. One time we met at LAX. I was flying home and he was flying out.

Finally, I let him know that I wanted to start a family. He didn't admit it, but I think that that thought terrified him more than anything. Neither one of us were good communicators, and we didn't know how to express our real feelings. We never wanted to hurt the other person and would rather say nothing than to say something that might be taken the wrong way. Even though I was twenty-six and he was thirty-one, when we married, neither one of us were mature adults who had learned to articulate our true emotions. We were a passionate love affair when we were together, but we both had so much growing up to do and, unfortunately, we had to do it while traveling to different destinations. We were more concerned with being professional in our working relationships than in our relationship with each other.

Soon after the episode with my parents, I competed in the World Professional Competition in Landover, Maryland, then went straight to the Proskate Competition in New York City. Directly from there, I caught a red-eye to San Francisco with my Nutcracker Prince, Olympic Champion Robin Cousins. We checked into an elegant boutique hotel for a two-hour sleep before a car picked me up to go to a television studio to tape the *A.M. San Francisco* show. Then we had our eleven o'clock dress rehearsal before our opening in *Nutcracker* at a two o'clock matinee that afternoon. This was my typical whirlwind schedule, and I was only gone for an hour and a half for the taping. But, as I stepped back into my hotel suite to get my rehearsal clothes, I immediately had a sinking feeling. Something didn't feel right; someone had been in there, rifling through my belongings. I had traveled hundreds of thousands of miles and stayed in hundreds of hotel rooms throughout my then-nearly-twenty-year career as a skater, but nothing had ever felt like this before. I soon discovered what was wrong. All my jewelry was missing.

I don't mean just a few pieces of jewelry I had brought to wear on this leg of my journey. I mean my entire collection. I was transporting the collection and, in the rush to get to the morning show, hadn't put my jewelry in the hotel safe. It was the one and only time I hadn't used a hotel safe. Everything was gone. My Van Cleef & Arpels pieces. Gone. My precious Radix pins. Gone. My ring that had been given to me by my father after I won the Olympics, a special piece custom-made with five gold bands twisted into the shape of the five Olympic rings. Gone. My piece from Jeanne Martin. Gone. Even my wedding band was gone.

A hasty, unsatisfactory investigation took

place. The housekeeper admitted that she had opened my room for a man while I was gone. I remembered a man asking for my autograph in Landover, Maryland.

"Nice jewelry you have on," he said admiringly.

"Thank you," I answered.

"So where are you off to next?" he asked.

"San Francisco. I'm doing *The Nutcracker,*" I said, without hesitation or reason for suspicion.

Because of an innkeeper's law still on the books in the city of San Francisco, I had no cause of action against the hotel. Since I had not availed myself of their safe, they were not liable for my loss, which totaled several hundreds of thousands of dollars. No detective followed through on the investigation, and the hotel didn't cooperate. I never felt they tried to do anything about it. They just allowed the housekeeper to unlock my room for a stranger — no questions asked. The housekeeper said she knew it was my room, but she opened it anyway. I felt violated. In addition to my expensive jewelry, many of the pieces were small tokens of my travels that could never be replaced. I called Dean. We always talked several times a day.

Dean was more than my husband, he was also my best friend. With his usual flair, humor, and compassion, he helped me through this difficult time. It was impossible for me to walk past jewelry stores without feeling angry and sad. I was irritable most of the time. After a while, I came to realize it was more than jewelry I had lost. I had lost what the jewelry represented. It was the only thing I had that was mine. And it brought me joy and made me feel good about myself. No one else had earned it and no one else could wear it. My deep hurt was slowly replaced with the rationale that all I had lost were material things. I had not lost a part of myself, even though sometimes it sure felt like I had. I needed to separate myself from what I thought the jewelry represented. I felt myself growing up in a major way and learned a life lesson few learn so young. I started to walk past jewelry stores and brush off the pang of the hurt associated with my loss when I realized I was putting too much emphasis on material things to define myself. It didn't happen quickly and it didn't happen overnight. But it happened.

The theft took a backseat to a much greater loss on February 4, 1983, when my friend Karen Carpenter died from a cardiac arrest after years of fighting anorexia. We had done two TV specials together, talked frequently on the phone, and we went to each other's performances as often as we could. I had last seen her just two months earlier when we were both staying at the Regency Hotel in New York. She had come to the city to get help from a physician specializing in eating disorders, and when she had knocked on my door, I hadn't recognized her. She'd weighed ninety-four pounds. When we talked, she'd told me how miserable she was without her family and how much she missed California, but she knew she had to stay in New York to get well. Then she'd handed me an article, I believe it was from *Life* magazine, written by her doctor.

"This is what I'm going through," she said.

Instead of describing to people the disease she was fighting, she would give this article to them, to explain it for her. I read it and tried hard to understand, but it was difficult for me. I couldn't fathom a skeleton-like thin person looking in a mirror and still believing she was overweight. But I tried my best to be empathetic because I loved her. I remembered walking into Jerry Weintraub's office and hearing him on the phone, "Do something about Karen. She's too skinny." I didn't know to whom he was talking, but it made me realize that everyone around her was concerned yet no one knew what to do to make it better. At that time, anorexia, like depression, was on the list of mysterious illnesses that no one dared to mention, let alone come to understand. Karen and I had no way of knowing that, at that moment in the Regency Hotel room, we were linked by societal ignorance. The worthless and hurtful answer to my family's history of depression was, "Keep your chin up," and to Karen's anorexia it was, "Just eat something."

In August of 1983, I took my sister, Marcia, with me to Sun Valley, Idaho, where I had been invited again to skate in one of their Saturday night shows. The setting of the show was spectacular, on their outdoor rink in front of the legendary Sun Valley Lodge. Marcia and I both had fond memories of Sun Valley. She had come with me to Sun Valley in 1976, when I had filmed one of my Clairol commercials, and had gotten an interview with the company at its headquarters near our hometown. She now worked for Clairol as a microbiologist. We had come a long way in building a sibling relationship that never had a chance to grow when we were children. She was becoming a friend whom I could trust. Because she had great insights into our parents' behavior, she was also becoming my bridge back to them.

Since my brother had moved away to Exeter at age twelve, it was she and I who had withstood our parents' fighting the longest. It was Marcia who had had to clean the entire house before Mom would return home from Colorado: If Mom walked into an unkempt home, she would have a temper tantrum. Marcia would always tell me she didn't mind our mother's long absences from home, as it enabled her to have the social life she craved, going to parties and dating more. I was so thankful Marcia didn't hold our family's unusual lifestyle against me.

After the Saturday night show, Marcia and I went our separate ways, she back to her life on the East Coast and me to my new Beverly Hills home with Dean. I knew something was wrong with Dean the second I walked into the house. He looked pale and distant. I asked him what was wrong. It wasn't until the next morning, after I made him his favorite breakfast, that he took me by the hand into the living room and declared:

"I don't want to be married anymore."

I was in shock. He continued.

"I still love you. You love me. That will not change."

I felt myself starting to crumble.

He knew I was crushed. We had been together for nine years. He packed his clothes within an hour and left. There was no one else I could talk to about it. He was my best friend, the only person I wanted to be with at this moment. I sat on our couch for two solid weeks and sobbed. Dean and I remained friends, and we continued to talk nearly every day. He was seeing a psychiatrist, and we decided I should go with him so I could find out why he couldn't be married anymore. We called it "marriage counseling," but I definitely had the disadvantage in these sessions, since the doctor knew Dean so well. They both told me it was important for Dean's ego to be the provider in our relationship. Dean felt he was not contributing enough. I'll never know if that was the actual reason. But that's what I was told. It was then that I decided that money must be evil. I was being penalized by everyone for making my own, first by my parents, then by Carlo Fassi, then by a jewelry thief, and now by my husband and his shrink. The psychiatrist made me feel that he didn't like me at all. It was obvious that I needed some other emotional support.

I called my sister to tell her, and she was devastated. She'd loved Dean from the moment she'd met him. When he'd come back with me to Connecticut to visit, he liked to jog around her neighborhood because he didn't feel like a celebrity in her town. He said when he got lost, all he had to do was ask somebody if they knew her husband, Bucky Blake, and he would be steered back to their home. He said Bucky was the celeb in these parts, not him, and he charmed everyone. But there wasn't much Marcia could do to ease my pain. She insisted I call my mother to tell her, I thought Mom would say, "I told you so," but when I talked to her I could feel the anguish in her voice. After her initial cold reception, she had come to love Dean and saw him as a member of our family. It was a time of crisis and I surprised myself. I flew home to be with my parents and my sister. The money issue took a backseat for all of us. My parents now saw only my pain and knew I needed them. They tried their best to comfort me, but the only person to whom I wanted to confide my feelings was the husband who no longer wanted me to be his wife. I had to face reality and realize that maybe my life was no longer in California. It was Dean and his family who had made it feel like home. Without him, I had no home. I purchased a house in Greenwich, Connecticut, to be near my family and to try to rebuild my life.

It turned out to be a nice bonding time for my family. My parents helped me with my new house, looking after it while I was out of town. My sister lived close by and continued to act as a necessary emotional bridge to my parents. I tried to pursue things I had been unable to do in my whirlwind lifestyle with Dean. I actually enrolled in sewing and cooking classes in nearby New Canaan. I had been around costumers for much of my skating career, and I was interested in knowing how they did it. I thought I could design some costumes, but I soon realized it would have helped if I knew how to draw. My sister joined me in the fun I'd always had baking, and I pulled out that Granola Date Coffee Cake recipe. It was so fattening we had to save it for one special time of the year. We began to make it as a Christmas morning tradition. It was hard to believe I once thought this gooey concoction was actually healthy, but, boy, is it good, and worth making for the pure guilty pleasure of it:

GRANOLA DATE COFFEE CAKE
Heat:
1 cup dates, chopped
1/2 cup water
1 tablespoon flour
Simmer in small saucepan for ten minutes.
Stir in:
1/2 teaspoon vanilla
(I put in a whole teaspoon.)
Then set aside.

In large bowl, cream:
1/2 cup of softened butter
2/3 cup of sugar
Beat in one egg.
Add in:
1 cup flour
1 teaspoon baking powder
1/2 teaspoon salt
Spread 1/2 of batter in an 8 x 8 greased glass pan and top with date mixture.

Then Make the Topping—
Smash until crumbly:
1/2 cup granola (where the granola finally comes in)
1/3 cup brown sugar
1/3 cup flour
2 tablespoons soft butter
Spread remaining batter over dates, then top with granola topping.
Bake 45 minutes at 300°F, until sides pull away from pan.

ENJOY!

I had been nominated for an Emmy in my role as Juliet in an ice production of *Romeo and Juliet* on CBS. It had been a fun project, and Dean and I were still married when I rehearsed it and shot it. I had a little experience skating pairs, but I wondered what it might be like to do it seriously. I found my most perfect Romeo in the funny, handsome, hardworking, easygoing Brian Pokar. Skating with him became a highlight of my career. It had aired on Thanksgiving 1982, and Dean was overjoyed when I was nominated in the spring. In no way was he jealous, although he was frustrated in his own career. He knew I didn't want to be an actress, but understood that it was important that I could convey the story of Juliet through my skating and that others in the industry appreciated it. When it came time for the Emmy Awards ceremony, Dean and I were separated. It felt unreal that the man who had encouraged me, mentored me, taught me how to deal with the limelight, the man whom I loved, was not beside me when my name was called and I went onstage to accept my Emmy. My emotions were on a roller coaster. My loneliness for Dean was palpable, but I was overjoyed to be chosen to win television's highest honor.

Thank goodness, I still had my skating. There was certainly a pattern to my life. When times were tough, I went skating. It was only while I was on the ice, enjoying the freedom of movement and my love of music, that I was able to escape from my bottomless heartache. Skating had always been my happy place and I certainly depended on it now. Dean insisted that he had to leave me because he felt he had lost his own identity. He didn't want to be known as Mr. Hamill, he joked. He said he didn't leave me for another woman, and I believe he had stayed faithful to me during our two-year marriage. Although women constantly threw themselves at him, he never made me feel he was interested in them. There were many times we would be having dinner and women would brazenly come up to him and give him their phone number, as if I were invisible. But he always took it in stride, shrugging it off and making it clear to me he was never interested in anyone but me. Still, I knew it fed his ego, as it would anyone's. Of course it bothered me, but ultimately I thought it was harmless. I discovered what truly fed his ego after an incident in Alaska. I took a group of skaters there for an exhibition — the show was called Skatefest Alaska. While there, I met a captain from Elmendorf Air Force Base.

"How would you like to come out to see the base?" he asked.

"I've seen Air Force bases, but if you can arrange a ride in an F-15, then I would love to visit," I answered. Of course I was joking!

I had visited several bases to see Dean fly and I had heard all the pilots' stories about how great it was to fly in an F-15. I'm not certain if the captain knew I was married to a fighter pilot or not. I was both joking and half serious. I wanted to feel what Dean and his flyboys felt every time they flew. Flying jet fighters was Dean's passion, just as skating was mine.

I skated in the show and forgot about my request. I never dreamed it would happen. Then I got the word from the captain.

"The flight for Ms. Hamill is a go. She has been cleared by the Pentagon."

My manager, Michael Rosenberg, was on the golf course in Anchorage when he learned, via walkie-talkie, of my impending flight, and his face went white. He didn't want anything to happen to his "racehorse."

I went up in the jet and I was on cloud nine. We flew around Mount McKinley and between the Cathedral Spires. Feeling the positive and negative g-forces was so powerful. We did rolls, Cuban eights, and max climb loops. It was the most thrilling experience of my life. The weightless twists and turns of the jet did nothing to upset my equilibrium, and the pilot attributed my sense of balance to my years of spinning and jumping. I couldn't wait to call Dean and tell him.

His response was unexpected. He felt I was gloating because he had never flown an F-15. The fighters he trained on were the smaller F-4s so I'm sure he was a little jealous. It was his dream and the dream of his buddies to fly in an F-15. All it took for me to get a ride was my request, while he had put in years of work toward this goal. He knew someday he would be able to get a ride but didn't know when. He had always had a need for speed, as he called it. He had bought a magnificent Porsche that had belonged to Steve McQueen. He had owned a helicopter and flown it, but that wasn't enough for him. He could have been a commercial pilot with his training, but that wouldn't have been enough for him either. He was determined to fly the fastest and most sophisticated piece of aircraft he could. And here I had ridden in something more advanced than he had ever flown, with one simple request. I wasn't about to apologize for taking this opportunity, and with time we started to bond over our shared joy of jet flying. He came to appreciate that I had done it because I wanted to feel closer to him. I could now understand the thrill of what he felt every day.

I was having trouble moving on after our breakup. It was difficult because we still talked on the phone nearly every day. I filed for divorce in the Santa Monica Court in the fall of 1983, but we still went out to dinner together like it was old times. We went on like this for nine months with the divorce not finalized: It was impossible for me to let this man leave my life. We talked about how the timing wasn't right for us. I was ready to get off the road and start a family. He was just starting to get back on his feet financially with his new career. He was also taking more time to see Alexander.

"I can't give you what you want right now, but someday we'll be together, no matter what," he'd say to me, tears filling his beautiful eyes.

A few months later, he landed his own starring role in a sitcom called *Misfits of Science,* playing the head of a group of superheroes who work for a think tank. He got his own apartment and enlisted the Martin family interior designer, Robert Scana, to decorate it. He said he wanted to try again with me and asked me to move into his apartment. He wanted to feel that he was supporting me. I didn't hesitate. We still owned the house in Beverly Hills, but if living in his apartment was important to him, I would gladly do it. I wanted to be with him. It didn't matter where we lived, as long as we were together.

He carried my things into his apartment, then announced that he had to do a celebrity bartending gig at a restaurant on Melrose called Gallagher's. We both went to Gallagher's with my manager and his wife, believing it would be a short evening and we would soon be back in our new home.

It wasn't to be. I had dinner with the Rosenbergs while Dean did his guest bartending. All evening long, I sat there and watched as several women flirted with him. And he flirted back. I sensed a change in his behavior that night. It made me wonder if he had ever cheated on me. I don't think any woman ever seeks out that kind of confirmation. But one time I got a hint of it. It came from my friend Kathy Porter.

Kathy had visited a fellow showgirl friend in Las Vegas and spotted something on her calendar. On one of the days, the friend had written, "Dino arrives" with hearts all around it. When Kathy questioned the girl, she batted her eyes as if she were completely in love.

That night at Gallagher's, the Rosenbergs saw my agony and proposed that we go to another restaurant for dessert. Dean had been told that he could leave, but he decided to continue working the bar. He suggested that I leave with the Rosenbergs and said that he would see me back at the apartment later.

But he never came home.

I don't have to be hit in the head twice. I finally got it. Our reconciliation didn't make it through one night. I guess he needed this episode as some sort of closure. It was over between us. I left the next morning and went back to our house. Our divorce was final in the spring of '84. Dean arrived at our court date dressed in a conservative navy blue suit with a white shirt and navy tie. He took my breath away. I never wanted to divorce this dear man. The judge asked if there was anything we wanted to say. Of course I had misgivings, but Dean said, "I'll do what you want."

He asked for no money. He said it was all mine, I had worked hard for it, and he didn't want anything.

And with that, our marriage was over.

Now I really did have to move on with my life. Feeling very sorry for myself, and still yearning for the beautiful life Dean and I would have had together, I tried to start doing again. But, I compared everyone to Dean. Then I heard that Dean had moved on to another skater. So I knew I had to somehow heal my heart.

I had a small getaway condominium in Palm Desert at the Rancho Las Palmas Country Club, and I decided to live there for a while even though I would have to contend with the hot summer desert sun. It turned out love was just a putting green away.

9
GOOD-BYE, DEAN

I never had the opportunity to learn golf, but I loved being around the endless green fairways, the flowers, the palm trees, and the boundless blue sky — probably because it was so different from my life of enclosed ice boxes. My condo was a short walk from the clubhouse, and I liked to go there for an iced tea. One day I spotted a man putting on the green whose looks set me back a breath. He was the spitting image of Dean. His blond hair swept back in a similar style, his aquiline nose was nearly identical, his eyes were set the same, and the profile of his chin seemed to match Dean's. At first I thought I might be imagining the similarity, but at second glance I realized it was true. My stomach felt slightly queasy at the sight. Michael Rosenberg was in town, and the two of them started talking out on the green. Michael called me over and introduced us.

Dean's lookalike was a man by the name of

Ken Forsythe, and he was a doctor of sports medicine. He lived in Santa Monica, but his father had a place at Rancho Las Palmas, and he had been visiting there for years to golf, swim, and play tennis. He was with his beautiful little daughter, Jennifer, and I assumed he was married. When Ken learned that Michael was a manager, he chatted up the book he had written about sports medicine and asked for Michael's help in selling it. That was the extent of our first meeting, and I did not think about him again except to mull over his likeness to Dean and my reaction to it. Could it be that I was still so much in love with Dean that I was projecting his good looks onto other men?

The next time I saw Ken was at the Rosenbergs' house back in Los Angeles. He was just leaving, while I was coming. He was there talking to Michael about more specifics concerning his book. We said hello and began talking — and I soon realized he was very funny and charming in a light, breezy way. He made no attempt to make a pass at me, and I still assumed that he was married. When he left, I asked Michael to elaborate on Ken. Michael only said that he thought Ken wanted to meet me. Since he had now done that, twice, I assumed that would be the extent of it for us.

Back in the desert, I would see Ken on the putting green from time to time and would nod hello. I was still learning to play tennis and was convinced that I must be the worst player in the world. I always went to the farthest court from the tennis house so that nobody could see how terrible I was. Ken was a tennis club champion, another similarity to Dean, and one day he was playing on the court next to me. I thought it was curious, since all the other courts nearer the clubhouse were open. Somebody that good would not be hiding out like me. Why was he playing over near me? I wondered. Later, he and Michael suddenly appeared on my condo doorstep in their golf carts. They were playing the course and wondered if I would like to ride along for the last two holes. I said sure, and hopped in the cart.

Along the way, Ken seemed so much more concerned about me than about his golf game. He asked me many smart questions about skating, challenging questions from a doctor's point of view, most of them concerned with health and fitness. He asked me if I would like to come to his clinic in Santa Monica to have my cholesterol tested. I said sure. I had always wanted to know more about health fitness and he was very athletic, so the next time I was back home in Los Angeles, I stopped at his clinic. I learned that my cholesterol was good. A couple of days later, he called me up and asked me out to dinner. Michael had said that he didn't think Ken was married, but I still said no. I thought it was too peculiar to date somebody who looked just like Dean. But I had made a pact with myself that I would date whoever asked me and not sit home feeling sorry for myself.

Tom Gees, the golf pro at the Rancho Las Palmas Club, asked me to a Kings game to see Wayne Gretzky play while he was still with the Oilers. At the game, Tom steadfastly insisted that Ken was very interested in me. I learned that he was separated from his wife. When he called to ask me out again, this time I said yes. Ken differentiated himself from other dates by taking me to a cozy, out-of-the-way restaurant. He didn't try to impress me. I liked that. I soon realized that he was a very nice person. I also thought he was intelligent, well-read, and knowledgeable. He had grown up in Canada and spoke the most proper English. He was the epitome of a gentleman to me, so considerate, thoughtful, and engaging at the same time.

Halfway through the dinner, Ken said both he and his soon-to-be-ex-wife were moving ahead quickly with their divorce. He also told me how he used to have a much larger medical clinic than the one I had seen, but he'd had to file for bankruptcy running that clinic and been forced to shut it down. He was attempting to do new and innovative work in sports medicine, and I liked his ideas. We had sports as our common ground, and it felt very comfortable.

Then, toward the end of the evening, he put his arm around me and, in that one moment, I felt more warmth emanating from this man than I ever had in a moment with Dean. Even though Dean claimed I was the "love of his life," his bouts of iciness had frequently left me feeling left out in the cold. Dean had never held me the way Ken did. I was looking forward to another date with this charming man.

At this time, I was training for the World Professional Competition, an event that I would eventually win five times in a row. But first, I had another engagement: a White House state dinner with Prince Charles and Princess Diana. Dean and I were still the best of friends, and we continued to speak regularly. He could tell I was falling for Ken, but I wouldn't admit to it. Still, I felt I had to tell Ken how I had asked Dean months earlier to accompany me to the White House. Ken didn't seem to have any problem with the fact I was going with my ex-husband. I explained that he was my best friend. And truthfully, Dean was always the perfect escort.

The enchanting Princess Diana was the centerpiece of the dinner. Every eye focused upon her. We couldn't help it, she was so beautiful and elegant. When we entered the dining room, I was told I could find my assigned dinner seat under the portrait of Lincoln. Couples were not seated together. When Dean and I entered the dining room, there was no one seated at my table, and I begged him to stand and wait with me so I wouldn't be alone. The dining room began to fill up. Soon every table was bustling with guests except for mine. It looked like I was going to be alone for dinner; it almost seemed like a mistake had been made. Still, Dean stayed by my side. Then President Reagan and Princess Diana entered the dining room together and a whisper swept over the room. They were heading toward my table!

"This is where I take my cue," Dean softly uttered, heading to his own table.

In an instant, I was surrounded by Princess Diana, President Reagan, David Hockney, Mikhail Baryshnikov, Leontyne Price, and Leonore Annenburg. Princess

Diana recalled how many times she had once stood outside Covent Garden waiting for Baryshnikov to appear, hoping for his autograph. The dinner conversation centered around the president and Princess Di, who wondered why the dignitaries, heads of state, and other notables who were invited to the White House and to Buckingham Palace felt compelled to take the silverware with them after they had eaten there. They were taking them as souvenirs, of course, but these two had found a common experience to share that no one else in the world could comprehend. It was amazing listening to them. The princess ate every morsel of her dinner and asked us what Johnny Carson was really like. As if we knew. Afterward, Mrs. Annenberg encouraged John Travolta to start the dancing. She led him to Diana, and they danced. It was sweet to watch the effect Diana had on the men in the room. Guests like Clint Eastwood, Tom Selleck, Neil Diamond, and Dean were men who could have any woman they wanted in the world, yet they turned into bashful, awestruck men. A couple of them finally mustered enough courage to ask her to dance, but it was John who seemed to capture her the most.

Dean and I went on to the World Professional Competition, where I won the Skater of the Year Award. It took me completely by surprise, and I became emotional because I had won it for my work with John Curry. The award meant so much to me, since it was given to me by my peers. I was grateful to have Dean there with me to share the joy this award evoked, yet the entire exciting trip didn't prompt us to rethink or revisit our married life. The trip's highlights, generated by my work, probably solidified in his own mind that he wanted to find his own claim to fame.

Ken and I continued to see each other back in Los Angeles, where I was busy choreographing upcoming shows and continuing to train for them. Then he asked me to go away with him at Christmas to Zermatt, envisioning us in horse-drawn carriages rustling through the snow-covered streets of the village. Wow; it made me think of all those years I'd wanted to take a romantic European vacation with Dean and how we could never make it happen. Sometimes, I'd go so far as to make the reservations and buy the tickets, but he would always find a reason to back out. It was something I had fantasized about, and I said yes. Ken had two children, Jennifer and Daniel, and he first took them to visit their mother in Sweden. I went to Paris for a professional competition, then took the train to Geneva to meet Ken. We had a wonderful time in Zermatt: He was so patient teaching me to ski that I actually did okay. He had played hockey in his native Canada, and went skating with me on the outdoor rink. We hiked, ate at great restaurants, and stayed in the most adorable hotel. We spent New Year's Eve there, and he was warm and fun to be with. It was there that I discovered I had fallen in love with him.

No one else in my life was happy for me. Michael Rosenberg told me Ken was an opportunist, but I knew that Michael felt any man coming into my life was a threat to his own career. He feared that I would settle down and have children. He told my parents about Ken's bankruptcy and divorce, and they assumed he was no good for me. My sister took an immediate dislike to him. He wasn't warm and funny to my family the way he was to me. He could be sarcastic, acerbic, and combative with them. He was very critical of Marcia because he felt she was overweight. My mom and sister banded together to express their dislike. I assumed it was because they loved Dean so much that they were not going to let anyone take his place. Still, my parents tried their best to accept Ken. They came and visited us in Palm

Springs and met with Ken's father and his wife. When Ken's children arrived, they babysat so that Ken and I could go out to dinner.

Ken was very supportive of my career and always made the effort to travel to see me. While I was performing at Harrah's Hotel in Lake Tahoe for a month, he brought his mother and children to visit. When I arrived back home, we caught an early dinner at the Moustache Café in Westwood.

"I have something to ask you," he said.

I was all ears.

"I was wondering what you thought of us getting married."

Taken by complete surprise, I nearly choked on my food. I knew his divorce was not yet final. But he continued to say all the right things — how much he loved me, how we were so great together. He was so romantic and I had such loving feelings for him. Yet I was very surprised.

"Sure, that would be great," I gushed.

Then he looked at the ring I was wearing. It was from Van Cleef & Arpels. After my entire jewelry collection had been stolen, I had indulged myself in only two nice pieces and this was one of them.

"I could never buy you a ring as beautiful as this one. So what if I went and had this one engraved?" he asked.

Sitting there and listening to him, it made sense. I said yes. Thus, my engagement ring became a ring I already owned.

Figuring that my mother would be pleased that I was going to marry a doctor, I learned her true feelings when she wrote friends and called him a quack. Dean was more forceful in his objection to my new choice of mate.

"He's no good, Dorothy. Watch out for this guy. He slept around on his wife when she was six months pregnant."

It sounded preposterous. "How would you know something like that!"

"I have my ways."

"I don't believe you."

"You don't want to believe me."

Dean had hurt me so deeply that it was impossible to trust that he was telling the truth about Ken.

"I'm moving on with my life, Dean."

Perhaps he did not hear conviction in my voice, but I did know I was never going to be able to have with Dean what I knew I could have with Ken — a family. I didn't see Dean's attempt at intervention as being protective. I felt he was being controlling. He didn't want me to be with anyone else, but he wouldn't commit to me only. Of course, I wanted to believe Dean was trying to stop me from marrying Ken out of a desire to have me again as his wife, but I knew that wasn't true and I couldn't beat myself up about it. There were so many times with Dean when we felt so much love that it hurt, and then other times when he would be so cold and distant and it would hurt just as much. With Ken I felt it was balanced, that I was both giving and receiving a steady stream of love, and that I was maturing with my new relationship.

It was time for Skatefest Alaska again, and we took the show up to Anchorage. Ken flew up with me. Appreciating it so much that he loved to travel with me, I turned to him and asked, "So when do you want to get married?

After thinking for a moment, he answered, "How about we do it in Alaska?"

One of the things I loved about Ken was his spontaneity. It was exciting to think that he was willing to get married so soon, but I didn't feel it was possible. He had answers for that too.

"We don't have to wait for blood tests in Alaska," he stated.

It made perfect sense to me that a doctor would know this bit of information.

"Maybe we could do it at Ben Tisdale's house," he went on.

Ben Tisdale was the promoter of the show in Alaska. He had become wealthy from the oil-clean-up business, and Ken had gotten to know him through me.

"Why don't I call him from Seattle and ask him?" We had a layover there, and now I had so much to think about before we arrived. He noticed my hesitation.

"This will be easy. No planning. No family drama."

"I already had the fairy-tale wedding. I don't feel I have to do it again," I said.

Ken had been married before, so he understood.

In the Seattle airport, I heard him on the phone with Ben Tisdale. "Dorothy and I were thinking about getting married on this trip and wondered if you knew of a good place in Anchorage."

He was quiet as he listened, then he grinned big, hung up, and turned to me. "Ben offered his house." Of course he had. Ken was very good at getting people to give him what he wanted. And he was very resourceful. Ben's next-door neighbor was a judge. When we got into town, Ben mentioned Judge Roberts would be happy to perform the ceremony.

My only job was to talk to Ben's wife about where I could order flowers and a cake on two days' notice. A reception had already been planned at their home for the skaters. Now it would become my wedding party. My best friend, who was a Canadian pairs champion, was my maid of honor. I had been her maid of honor. We had Michael Siebert and Judy Blumberg, national dance champions and Olympians, and now traveling with Skatefest, in the wedding. The affair was so rushed that there was no time for any family members to fly up. Perhaps that was intentional, because none of mine were supporting me in my choice of Ken. I felt so happy, but they didn't want to accept it.

The ceremony was planned for sunset because the Tisdale house had huge windows overlooking Anchorage that beautifully captured the setting sun. When the rest of the cast and crew arrived for the planned party, they learned they were in for a surprise: They were here for my wedding reception! Richard Dwyer and Karen Kresge, the skaters whom I had idolized as a little girl watching Ice Follies, were also in our show. Now they were guests at my wedding. I had packed one dress for this trip, a black velvet cocktail dress fit for the Alaskan winter. There was no time to rush out and buy something else. So that's why I wore black to my wedding: It should have been an omen. It was March 5, 1987, only a year and a half after my divorce from Dean had become final.

Two days after the wedding, Ken pulled Judge Roberts aside and asked if he could make him an American citizen. We had no honeymoon and instead flew back to Palm Springs, where Ken promptly ruptured his Achilles tendon playing tennis. He had his foot put in a cast, couldn't walk, and was housebound, laid up on the couch.

Only two weeks later, on March 21, I got a call from Dean's good friend, Scott Sandler. He was on his car phone and he sounded desperate.

"Dorothy, I have some bad news about Dean."

"What? What is it?" My stomach seemed to rise up to my throat.

"I wanted you to hear this before you heard it on the news. Dean was on a routine training mission out of March Air Force Base, and his plane has gone missing."

"Missing! What do you mean?"

"The last the controller heard was a request to ascend. The request was denied, I don't know why, and they don't know where he is."

There was no way this was happening.

Even though Dean absolutely believed in the pilot code never to abandon his plane, I had heard him once joke that he would bail out if something went wrong. Now I was hanging on to that sliver of hope.

I immediately thought of his beautiful son. "Where's Alex?"

"Alex is with me. We are heading to Jeanne's house. Alex and I had gone with him to the base. We watched him go up."

Tears filled my eyes. Alex was only fourteen years old.

"Look, I have to go now. But I'll keep you informed," Scott said.

We hung up, and I felt dizzy as I turned on the news.

"Are you all right?" Ken asked.

"Dean is missing. He was flying . . ." I trailed off, in shock, as the TV news rattled on impassively, "Permission had been given by March Air Force for Martin's F-4 Phantom to perform a 'maximum climb takeoff.' The aircraft was seen disappearing into a scattered cloud ceiling at forty-seven hundred feet. Radar contact was lost nine minutes into the flight."

Ken turned ashen at the news. "It's astonishing that the base has no idea where Dean is."

We kept the phone lines open for any more

news. Scott and I talked numerous times that day and in the next four days as they searched for Dean. Was he dead or alive? Many people were calling, wanting news or offering news. His siblings hired a psychic, who pointed them to the San Gorgonio Mountains. There was an added urgency to finding him because there was a deep snow cover in those mountains. Even if Dean's survived a crash, could he survive the freezing temperatures?

Finally, on March 25, the burnt wreckage was spotted from the air by the rescue team. The crash site was five miles southeast from Mount San Gorgonio. Dean's remains and those of his weapons systems officer, thirty-nine-year-old Captain Ramon Ortiz of Las Vegas, were recovered.

An investigation revealed that the aircraft had flown upside down into a solid wall of granite between the two peaks of Wood Canyon, at an altitude of 3,750 feet and at the estimated impact speed of 560 miles per hour. Dean's jet had been in a formation of three that were under the control of civilian air-traffic controllers at Ontario International Airport. The Ontario ATC had instructed all three pilots to turn left to avoid the 11,502 summit of Mount San Gorgonio. The other two pilots had complied, but

Dean's jet had been caught in a dense cloud cover that affected his ability to know his position and altitude. Further investigation concluded that the maximum climb takeoff required by the fighters and the ensuing g-forces caused by it, combined with the cloud cover, disoriented him so that he didn't know his aircraft's position in relation to the surrounding terrain.

Mount San Gorgonio is one of the highest peaks surrounding Palm Springs; I could see it from my porch outside my door. I couldn't look at it. Ken was supportive throughout and told me to do whatever it was that I needed to do. I needed to get to Los Angeles. I jumped into the car and drove to Dean's apartment. When I saw his prized car parked there, I just sat crying. Dean's neighbor came out. I didn't know this woman, but she was crying, telling me how sorry she felt. My sister and parents had called as soon as they'd heard. They were devastated. My sister knew how much I loved Dean.

According to Scott, while Dean had been waiting for weather clearance, a woman who worked at the base had asked him what he thought about my recent marriage. He didn't know I had gotten married.

He'd turned to her, his face in shock, and

reacted incredulously. "She did?"

The wedding had been so impulsive that I hadn't had a chance to tell him beforehand. When we returned from Alaska, I'd had another week on tour before returning to the desert. I was so busy taking care of Ken, because of his incapacitating injury, that I'd never had a chance to call Dean and tell him. I wanted to tell him in person; he deserved to hear it straight from me. The fact that he'd had to hear it from somebody else, and immediately before he was to command an F-4 in the air, haunts me to this day.

I was uncertain how the Martin family felt about me and if I still had a place in their hearts, especially with their grieving. Dean had been tight-lipped about other women he was seeing, and I didn't want to make the Martin family uncomfortable by expecting to still have a place among them. At the funeral, I stood to the side, trying not to be noticed. It was a beautiful service at the Los Angeles National Cemetery, befitting a man who unselfishly gave his life in the service of our country. James Woods spoke eloquently of his friend. There was a missing-man formation flyover. When the American flag was folded, it was given to Alex.

Afterward, I went to Dean Sr.'s house. It

was comforting to be back with Dean's family and buddies, and we shared memories of him. Dean Sr. was very quiet. After a while, he went into his room alone. I felt like Dean's widow, but I didn't know if others realized it. How could they? It seemed I had moved on. But if Dean and I had still been married, I don't think I could have hurt any more than I did. Scott had told me that he once asked Dean if he thought he could be monogamous. The answer didn't really surprise me. Dean told him he really didn't think so. Strangely, I took solace in this confession. It wasn't me he had rejected; it was the institution of marriage.

It was pure heartache stepping back into our Beverly Hills home. I had bought this house with Dean, and we had wonderful memories there. When I found the pilot's helmet Dean had given me, signed, "To my co-pilot in life," I knew I couldn't live in this house anymore. Ken suggested that I sell it to buy a home in the Palm Springs area, and I knew the only thing I could do was to make my home someplace else. Los Angeles and life were forever changed for me. Maybe I thought moving away was the only way I could survive the tragedy of losing Dean. But no matter what I do or where

I go, I can never escape the loss.

To this day, I still see Dean in my dreams. These vivid dreams are so realistic that when I wake up, I believe he has been there with me and that he is still alive. I remember the precious moments of these dreams and how clearly he is talking to me. He tells me not to worry about him and that he is all right. He speaks to me in these dreams:

"The time isn't right now, but someday we will be together."

"I've just been hiding out."

"The reason we're not together is not because I don't love you."

"Don't worry. I'm here."

"We will be together. But not now. I had to go away."

For these dream-filled moments, I feel I can live because he is here with me. I wake up feeling wonderful. But when I resume full consciousness, I realize it was just a dream and am always devastated to realize he's not there. I fight my depression when I have to face the truth every day. Sometimes I find myself talking to Dean to get through these days and I feel his presence around me. When we were together, we talked about dying young. I said I wasn't able to envision us growing old together. I told him I had a gut feeling I would die at a young age. I never imagined Dean would be the one to die young. It is a chapter of my life that I am unable to close.

10
FAMILY LIFE . . . FINALLY

Ken and I found a new spec home in Indian Wells, off of Fairway Drive, that was almost completed, and we were able to pick out the finishing touches. From this house, I could see the mountain where Dean had died. I don't know if I was finding comfort in that or not. My anger over his death was not subsiding. I continually wondered, why him? He was somebody who was trying so hard to find himself. He didn't have to find it on the side of a mountain.

Fighting to stay in the present and get on with my life, I discussed with Ken the fact that Palm Springs was a simpler and perhaps better place to raise a family. We were ecstatic when I became pregnant in December of that year. I felt I had a very nice and comfortable home life and that I was truly starting over.

I had a horrible pregnancy. Nauseous for nine and a half months (I went two weeks overdue), I lost fourteen pounds in the first trimester and was so dehydrated I began hallucinating. Scheduled to skate in the closing ceremonies of the 1988 Olympics, the infamous Battle of the Brians, I went to the rink every day to stay in shape. When I got to Calgary, I threw up during practice sessions, then on the gigantic ice surface in the stadium. Luckily, I dashed to find a garbage can just in time. My stomach began growing so quickly that I barely fit into my dress for the exhibition. Thankfully, during the closing ceremonies, even though I was dizzy from the spotlights, I managed to finish the number without actually being sick. I'd go out to dinner and wouldn't understand the menu. I'd see the word cheeseburger, but I couldn't picture what a cheeseburger looked like. It was a very strange experience.

Meanwhile, Ken was doing a behind-the-scenes investigative look at doping in the Olympics. My new agent had helped Ken get this work, using his sports medicine background, but Ken was ahead of his time. It was something he was passionate about, but to the International Olympic Committee, he was too passionate. They were worried about the negative publicity and only aired one of his pieces.

Back home, I continued my workouts and

tried to stay in shape. The nausea never subsided. I was in the throes of depression from Dean's death, but I never had a chance to understand its symptoms because I was so sick. I even threw up on the day I delivered. Since I was two and a half weeks past my due date, I was very uncomfortable.

I felt like I couldn't take a break from work to enjoy my pregnancy and then I worried about it after I delivered. How was I going to take time to enjoy being a mother when I would have to work so hard to earn a living? I couldn't figure out why Ken had not really worked since our wedding day. He had given up his work at the Santa Monica Clinic when we moved to Indian Wells full-time. He had grandiose ideas of things he wanted to do, and I believed in him, even though I hadn't seen solid evidence that any of his plans could bear fruit. We had joined Mission Hills Country Club, and he played golf every day. He was already leading a retirement lifestyle, and I hadn't even given birth yet.

Finally, I started having contractions and went to the hospital. It was on the Friday nearly three weeks after my due date. But I wasn't dilated enough and was sent home. On Sunday, the contractions were stronger, but my obstetrician sent me home again, telling me to come in Monday morning and we would induce labor. Over the weekend, I remember passing my baby's nursery and becoming scared. All these contractions and nothing was happening. What did it mean? I was worried about my baby. I paged Ken on the golf course and anxiously asked if he thought everything was going to be okay. He was a doctor and a father who had been through childbirth with his ex-wife. He managed to comfort me and insisted everything would be fine.

By ten the next morning, I was back in the hospital; the doctor had to break my water, and I was put on Pitocin to intensify the already fierce contractions. I was given a bit of Demerol to help with the pain. The nurses and staff were surprised at my stamina over the many days of contractions. I knew my athletic training was helping me through it. I wasn't trying to be superwoman; I just wanted a natural birth and feared having to go in for a C-section. I insisted to Ken and my OB that as long as the baby was fine, I was going to have a vaginal birth.

After twelve more hours of contractions, my baby's heartbeat started slowing down, and Ken told me the baby had to come out now. They were going to have to do a C-section. They rolled me into surgery, and I gave it one more try. The anesthetist pushed down on me and finally the baby's head crowned. They were able to get the suction on her head and pull her out. The reason she wasn't delivering was because her head was so big. She had been stuck. We lovingly called her "Blockhead" for a long time. She was beautiful and healthy, and we named her Alexandra. Ken and I knew we wanted a name that fit a boy or a girl. Alex was the only name we both liked.

I loved how my whole world changed the minute she was born. The world was new for me just as it was for her. The minute I finished with labor, I wanted to go straight home with her. The staff was amused and said they had to keep me until the morning. I just wanted to hold her. I felt love like I had never known, a love impossible to describe.

Marcia had delivered her second daughter, Becky, just one week earlier. We were elated to share our joy with each other. Marcia's joy brought tears to my eyes because she had lost her baby boy in her seventh month five years before.

It was so lovely being with Alex, and she was such an easy baby. She fell asleep easily, woke up easily, and ate well. When I heard parents complain about their tough baby years, I couldn't possibly know what they were talking about. Every moment of my day with Alex was the most beautiful thing I had ever experienced. Most of the time, I just stared at her. So innocent, so sweet. Her movements and sounds, her first smile, her first cooing, her beautiful eyes, were all sources of endless joy for me. Dick Button sent her a pair of double-runner ice skates, and Harlick, the skate boot company, sent the smallest pair they made. Ken was so good with her, and I was so happy he already had practice with babies. He was adept at feeding and changing diapers. It meant that I could relax and know she was safe. I even brought Alex to the mall with me. It had been months since I had skated. I was determined to make it to the Landover, Maryland, Capitol Center to compete at the Nutrasweet World Professional Championships, since I had won it five times in a row since 1983. Wanting to defend my title, I gave my choreographer and dear friend a call and told her of my plans. I was dismayed at her reaction.

"Oh, Dorothy, what do you want to do that for?" It was a knife in my heart. Her deprecating tone was clear: I was silly to think I could compete after having a baby. That was her way of telling me she had moved on to the hot skaters, like Katarina Witt and Brian Boitano.

"I want to challenge myself," I stammered.

She made me feel I was suddenly old news, past my prime. I was not in a position financially to retire! I had never had such a lengthy downtime. The fall and winter were the seasons for me to earn a living, and I wanted to get back to work.

"Actually, I was hoping you would choreograph my programs." I suddenly felt sheepish asking my very good friend to do this for me. She hesitantly said yes.

Alex was less than two months old when I packed her up and traveled from sunny Palm Springs to freezing cold Toronto. It seemed perfectly natural to me to pick up my daughter and pick up my skates as I walked through the airports. I was still nursing. I had brought along a nanny, Raffaela, who spoke no English and who was an acquaintance of Ken's. Ken spoke fluent Spanish and had found Raffaela through an office employee. Her name was Maria. Maria had become my friend, and I felt I could trust Raffaela because of Maria's recommendation.

My friend reluctantly choreographed two programs for me, and they were not difficult. I was easily landing double lutzes before my pregnancy. Now the toughest jump I could count on was my double toe — curiously, the jump I had taught myself. My choreographer and I had been each other's maid of honor. Our friendship had started when we were young in Lake Placid together. She had been at the forefront of the changing face of the professional ice show when audiences began to become more sophisticated about skating, demanding to see the headliners seen on televised world competitions. She had choreographed my numbers for Stars on Ice. The show had such skating stars as Robin Cousins, Toller Cranston, Blumberg and Siefert, and Paul Martini and Barbara Underhill. Now she was making me feel washed up.

I was very unsure of myself. Irina Rodnina, the Russian pair champion, had had a baby in 1980, just six months before she won the Olympics. But the skating world had treated that as an almost freakish anomaly, something only the tough Russians were capable of doing. I had no American counterpoint to Irina to serve as my role model. I knew it wasn't the end for me just because I had given birth, but most others seemed to have thought so. Ken flew in for the competition and made me feel more positive about my abilities. He put on a good show for everybody. He was affable, charming, and convinced of my prowess. I placed fourth. The others were all younger than I. And childless. I was simply happy to be able to fit into my costume!

Our new family, Ken, Alex, myself, and "Raffa" went straight to Paris for another competition, the European version of the Nutrasweet event. It felt very natural to be back on the ice, although I was still very rusty. We had so much fun in Paris, strolling three-month-old Alex around the Eiffel Tower. I skated with her for the first time, holding her close to me. This might have troubled some people, but I was more comfortable skating than walking!

We were a blissfully fulfilled family. I felt I had it all. Ken and I were happy, and we had a wonderful daughter. What more could a woman want? We decided to spend Christmas in our own home, just the three of us — "baby's first Christmas." I had been going home for Christmas nearly every year. My parents had to understand I could no longer do that. The Granola Date Coffee Cake was baked at our house that year.

Christmastime has always been special to me. I had performed the part of Clara in two *Nutcracker* productions in San Francisco during the month of December, back in

1981 and 1982. I had never had any creative input into those productions, and over the ensuing years, I had become interested in producing, especially after working with John Curry. I felt frustrated with the lack of quality production in many of the shows I had skated in. I wanted to put together my own *Nutcracker*. It was a natural combination of music, skating, and a familiar story, and not too big of a leap to pull off financially. First, I went in search of an original choreographer who would bring freshness both to *The Nutcracker* and to skating. I wanted someone skilled in musical staging and found her in Deedee Wood, who had choreographed *Mary Poppins*. She came in working with Nathan Birch, who had successfully combined ice and ballet while working with John Curry. John Curry was back home, living with his elderly mother, keeping a low profile, and we thought maybe he was ill. But nobody knew with what.

When Gary Beacom signed on to play the Prince, my partner in the show, I knew we could have a successful run. He was the 1988 World Professional Men's Champion and an innovative skater who was sought after by all the top show producers. He was a genius on and off the ice, with a double major in philosophy and physics from the

University of Toronto. Gary and I, and the remainder of the cast, the strongest set of skaters I could hire, gathered in Palm Springs for rehearsals. We began at eleven each night at the Town Center Mall rink, competing with the disco sound from the nearby Red Onion Restaurant. It was tough interpreting Tchaikovsky's "Nutcracker March" over the ranting beat of "Love Shack," but we used it to our advantage to help keep the skating fresh.

We performed at the Minneapolis Orpheum Theater for the month between Thanksgiving and Christmas. Skating with other strong skaters and playing a role were a dream come true for me. I truly did have it all. It was such a wonderful experience for everyone, most of all for Ken and me personally. We did it a second year. This time we performed it in Minneapolis and Chicago. The show was taped for NBC. I felt the second year was better than the first because we had more experience. It was a labor of love as we took a greater leap financially. It was worth the investment, because it was more satisfying to embody a role for two hours than to skate for three or four minutes, then disappear behind a curtain for the next hour. In *The Nutcracker* my role was woven in throughout the show's entirety. By the end, when we took our bows, I found myself truly enjoying the applause, not for me, but for the quality of the show.

My endorsement schedule kept me very busy, working with Bausch & Lomb and doing Healthy Choice commercials. Alex appeared in a few commercials with me. Ken kept dreaming up his business ideas, but none were panning out. He had developed a sports drink, and he wrote software for a back rehabilitation table he had invented. Then he began to assert himself in the business side of my skating career. He had been inspired while sitting in the audience at *The Nutcracker* and witnessing a Vikings football player, enjoying a Christmas outing with his family, jump to his feet, cheering, "This is the best thing I've ever seen!"

The huge football player was obviously not a typical ice-show audience member, and Ken saw hope in the mass appeal of these kinds of ice shows. He thought there could be twenty *Nutcracker*s playing around the country in the month of December. He said skating was a beautiful sport and changes should be made within it to change with the times. He was very enthusiastic about believing that the audience was ready for the sport to emerge in a bigger way. He was right. But I knew twenty different companies of *The*

Nutcracker was not the way for it to change.

To get any of Ken's previous ideas established would have cost too much. But he wanted me to invest in his ideas, and after hearing one after another, I finally did. He gave a business plan to my new accountant, Steve Mansfield, that we both liked. Ken wanted to start a company called "Check-up Express." The concept was to monitor key parameters of one's health — cholesterol, blood pressure, and body fat — by putting kiosks in malls. He hired workers to build the expensive kiosks and bought state-of-the-art pieces of medical equipment to put in them. Ken set them up in malls and kept track of them. He opened an office and hired our friend, Maria, as his assistant. She worked very hard for the enterprise.

Steve Mansfield handled all my bills, and one day he brought me an envelope. We were standing in the kitchen in Indian Wells.

"You should look at this."

I opened it. It was a bill from a law firm whose name I did not recognize. It was for legal services relating to Ken's divorce.

"What does this have to do with me?" I asked Steve. Steve was just getting to know Ken and me. I liked Steve and was growing to trust him because he did things differently from other accountants who had betrayed me. I was becoming older and, hopefully, wiser when dealing with my finances. I had Steve send me a monthly statement and made sure I signed all my checks.

"He has no income and can't pay this bill. And you are now married to him," Steve said.

Ken walked into the kitchen. He saw the bill. I could feel the unhappiness sweep over him, and I wanted it to go away. I didn't want to make an issue of it and have it be something that came between us. We knew the law firm would continue to pressure Ken to pay this bill. They knew we were married. So it became my responsibility. I had no choice but to pay it.

"Don't worry about it," I said to Ken, and gave Steve the go-ahead to make out the check.

I had already been paying Ken's child support and alimony payments after his own money had run out. Paying his legal bills didn't seem far afield.

Ken had begun to switch his focus onto other ideas once he set up Check-up Express. The company quickly began to lose money, yet we had to continue to keep up the leases on the kiosk installations. Steve finally said, "You have to get rid of this." Steve told Ken to find a buyer, but all he could do was to sell the medical equipment from the kiosks.

Meanwhile, I was discovering that Ken was good with Alex for only short periods of time. He'd do active things with her, like swim or hike, but caring for her needs bored him. When Jennifer and Daniel came to visit, he would be the same way, never altering his life to yield to them. He'd take them golfing, to play tennis, or to work out at the gym, as long as it was what he wanted to do. The children were not athletic fanatics like their father. Rarely were they up for eighteen holes of golf. He spent less and less time with them; I was the one to take care of them. When they showed an interest in horseback riding, I set up the lessons, drove them there, and made sure they were all right. I didn't mind, but they would be angry because they had traveled all the way from Sweden to spend time with their father, not with me.

In 1992, I was hired to be the special guest star of Ice Capades, meeting up with the tour in select cities. I was now thirty-six years old. Ken learned that Ice Capades was in bankruptcy court and suggested that we buy it. He felt we could get it for cents on the dollar and run it better. It was a great trademark; it just needed some fresh ideas. I told him there was no way we could afford to buy Ice Capades.

"Let's talk to Ben," he answered.

Ben was the promoter of my Skatefest tours in Alaska. Not only did I already have a great working relationship with him for four years running, but Ken and I still had fond memories of how he had opened his home for us to get married. Ken and Ben were like old friends. Ben had gone on to earn a fortune with his company, Martech, since it held many patents on oil-clean-up operations. Ken reminded me how much I loved producing *The Nutcracker* and how I could possibly take that kind of creativity and responsibility to a new level. He made me believe I could do it.

"Sure. Sounds great," I said, and I told him to call Ben.

11
ESCAPADES

Ben came on board, and we bought Ice Capades for 2.3 million dollars from the bankruptcy court. The price tag may have seemed high for what little was left of their inventory. Most of it, from costumes to real estate, had disappeared with previous owners and employees. But we thought it was a bargain because it meant we had all their venue dates. The most complicated part of the live-touring business is logistics and scheduling arena dates. Arena contracts don't allow overlapping with or backing up against other ice shows: There isn't enough business to go around. Our secured dates at the best venues meant that no other touring companies could get our routing. Having these dates assured us that no family show could be booked thirty days before or thirty days after Ice Capades. It was a brand name that was worth far more than a few costumes.

Besides, Ken and I were starting anew with

a different concept in professional ice shows. We felt our biggest competition, if at all, was Ken Feld. He had bought Ice Follies, then licensed all the Disney titles children were growing to love, *Beauty and the Beast, The Little Mermaid, Aladdin, Pocahontas,* and on and on. Young Alex had always loved these shows. *Beauty and the Beast* was huge; it confirmed that audiences wanted to be enchanted with a story when they came to an ice show. I knew I loved telling a story with skating because of my experience with *Nutcracker.* We wanted to produce a theatrical show emphasizing elite-level skating and felt we would serve a different market than Disney on Ice, which was geared toward very young children. We felt that there was room for both our shows. We signed the deal in New York, and it was supposed to be kept secret. We took Alex to see *Beauty and the Beast,* and we were surprised when Ken Feld came out to greet us.

"I heard you bought Ice Capades," he said without first saying hello. We had never formally met.

"We're here to see your show. Our daughter's a big fan. Nice to meet you, Mr. Feld."

"Hello, I'm Ken Feld," he said, and he kindly put out his hand.

We enjoyed the show, but it also assured us

that what we wanted to do was different. First, we picked "Cinderella" as the story because we felt this would appeal to families of all ages and not just little children. We gave it an original twist and entitled it *Cinderella: Frozen in Time*. We hired a composer to write an original score. This meant that each skater would be skating to music specifically composed for his or her character, a dream of many skaters. Then we set about to find the best skaters we could. Auditions were held, and we had difficulty choosing. We needed skaters who could land double Axels as well as do ensemble skating. We hired many skaters previously working with the show. We committed to higher salaries for the skaters and nicer hotels to stay in. We only allowed the maximum of two skaters to a room, as opposed to the tradition of cramming in four or more. I got rid of the humiliating weekly weigh-ins because they were unnecessary. Since we had top-notch skaters, I knew they were all most concerned about staying in shape to skate their best. They didn't need to step on a scale to prove it to a performance director. These were all things I wanted for myself when I had been with Ice Capades for eight years and I wanted to see other skaters get them.

It was rewarding to see the results. Our

high expectations meant that the skaters practiced more and took pride in their work. They each loved developing a character to portray without hiding inside an animal head. They relished working with the original compositions. A highlight was the recording of our original music with Sinfonia of London, comprised of musicians who were the first chairs of the London Symphony and the Royal Philharmonic. They were an amazingly talented group of people, truly the best of the best, who came together for recordings only. At my invitation, my parents eagerly flew over to witness the recording. I knew my father would particularly appreciate it, but his reaction was more touching than I expected. He broke down in tears of joy. He was so emotional he could not leave the recording studio. I was so proud that I had created this moment for him. It remains a highlight of my career.

The choreography was based on British pantomime and embellished on the broad motions of what we called "ice acting." I know Dean would have loved what we were trying to do, remembering how he had connected to John Curry's vision. I was trying to set a new standard and a new image for figure skating. I didn't buy the show so that I could give myself a job skating for the rest of my life. I didn't want it to be about me. I wanted it to stand on its own, providing family entertainment with world-class skating. The choreography showed great skaters skating as one.

We had two companies, East and West. Each show had a cast of thirty skaters and a crew of thirty more. We weren't sure audiences would take to our show. We all believed in it, but didn't know how people would respond. Our competition was very curious as to what we were doing and on opening night sent people to find out.

Our opening night was in Tulsa, Oklahoma, my home for a summer when I'd first started out with Carlo. Here I was, twenty-one years later, owning a major ice show. When we reached the intermission, as Cinderella is on her way to the ball in the carriage and the snow is falling, we received a standing ovation. No other skater in the troupe had ever received such a thunderous, appreciative reaction — a standing ovation at intermission! It was more acceptance than we could possibly imagine. The applause gave us all goose bumps.

"Can you believe this?!" We hugged each other backstage; some of us were crying.

We received rave reviews in every city we played. They couldn't have been better reviews if we had written them ourselves. In years past, it had been impossible to get a review on an ice show because they weren't taken seriously by either the entertainment or sports communities. But now it was different. It was exhilarating to know that people understood what we were trying to do and that it was appreciated. Ticket sales were way up. Audiences loved us.

Ken Feld started advising venues that he wasn't going to bring his show to them if they continued to book Ice Capades. Even though we had contracts with the venues, they chose Disney on Ice over us because it was the more established show. We lost our strongest markets. It hurt our bottom line, but we were on such a high we hoped to make up for it.

Unfortunately, our euphoria was short-lived. The day we opened in Los Angeles, it was announced on the front page of the *Wall Street Journal* that Ben Tisdale, our sole financial backer, was being investigated for the government contracts he had signed for his company, Martech. Ben assured us that his other company had nothing to do with us and that we were small potatoes compared to his other financial dealings. He was making millions from patents he had won in his environmental clean-up businesses. *Fortune* magazine had just named his company number sixteen on its list of the top one hundred small companies in the country.

But the stories about his company continued to run almost constantly in the *Wall Street Journal*. Stockholders were suing him. It was making our vendors — for instance, those selling programs and advertising — very nervous, and they began to demand their payments upfront. Ben came to us and asked us to find someone to buy him out.

We continued to keep the show on an even keel while we began to look for a buyer. We played our venue dates and taped the show for Sony. We were maintaining ticket sales levels, but we needed the upfront money to start developing the next year's show. That meant salaries for composers, costume designers, musicians, recording engineers, choreographers, and funds to secure contracts for the best skaters. It also meant that we could not procrastinate, as there was necessary lead-time to do everything from developing the story and theme all the way through to planning the advertising and shooting our commercials. There was immense pressure, not only to find a buyer fast in order to start on next year's show, but from Ben himself, who wanted out immediately. We had been worried about Ben's health. He was overweight, and Ken had been working with him to lose some of it. Now the jolly businessman whom we thought we knew so well was getting more and more tense. He was insistent that we look at the offer on the table from the Family Channel, which was owned by Pat Robertson.

The Family Channel flew Ken and me to Virginia Beach, to Regent University, to meet Pat Robertson's son, Tim. I thought we had arrived at the Stepford of universities. It didn't seem real: It was so clean and perfect, and there were only men on the campus. They put us up in the luxurious Founders Inn, a Georgian-style resort, complete with formal gardens and fitness facilities, and wined and dined us with opulent lunches and dinners. All the people we met with seemed so nice as they politely expressed how the merging of Ice Capades into their world would be "synergistic." But I was concerned that they didn't know anything about skating, and had never done a live touring arena show. I'd been touring in live shows for twenty years, and I wanted to hand over the show to experienced people. They took us to a taping of *The 700 Club* and we met very briefly with Pat Robertson.

The pressure to sell was overwhelming.

Ben would not front the money for the next year's show, so I started funding it myself. Lawyers assured me that I would get my investment back when I signed the deal with the Family Channel. So I agreed to the sale. We had purchased an airplane hangar in Arizona earlier in the year and made our own ice rink where we could choreograph, rehearse, shoot photographs for the program, and film our commercials. With the success of *Cinderella,* we decided to tell another fairy tale, "Hansel and Gretel." Alex was now five years old, and we enrolled her in kindergarten in Arizona.

The deal was taking a very long time to close. I was forced to put in more and more money to keep the show going. We went to London to record the music with Sinfonia, but it wasn't quite the same joyful experience we had had the year before because we seemed to have a gun to our heads. Tim Murphy, our choreographer, had to hand-carry the master recording from London back to the States. I was feeding the machine all the money I had and no longer taking a salary myself. I lost it one day and screamed at the lawyer, "I can't keep this up! What makes you so sure I'll get my money back?" There was something about these people I didn't trust.

So much of the financial business was falling on my shoulders that I couldn't keep an eye on the creative part of the show, which was my strength. I knew there were some parts of the show that worked and some that didn't, but I never grasped the flow of it because I never had the chance to sit out in the audience and watch it. In between my numbers, I was dealing with getting the snow machine fixed or talking with lawyers. In addition to the eight shows I performed each week, I had to continue to do PR. There was so much stress that I became very ill. I'd never had asthma before, but suddenly my breathing sounded like I had a harmonica in my lungs, the result of a cold that refused to go away. The worst part of all was that I had so little time to spend with my sweet daughter. While she was always with me, I could never focus only on her. I had never expected to carry the burden of the entire show when I'd first started on this venture. This was not how I wanted to lead my life. I was stuck.

What kept me going was the joy I felt working with the skaters. We had found the most phenomenal skaters in the world and knew other shows were trying to steal them from us. We paid them double what they might get at another show, to keep them on, and treated them very well. I always made sure they were paid, because they meant so much to me. I wasn't about to leave them high and dry like so many others had done.

Then, on January 5, 1994, I broke a rib. My ribs had been continually bruised throughout the length of my stint as Cinderella from the lifting by my partner, Andrew Naylor. At the beginning of the second act, our timing was off a fraction of a second going into a swan position, and he had to hook around, leaning hard to avoid the edge of the ice. Skaters move at such a fast speed that the slightest mistake can cause injury. I suddenly heard a *pop* and couldn't breathe. The clock struck midnight and I scurried off the ice. I whispered to my Fairy Godmother:

"I think I broke my rib."

I finished the show in agonizing pain, hardly able to breathe. The next morning, I went to a clinic for an X-ray. I had a stress fracture. The extra tight squeeze from my partner had caused it to snap.

Later that afternoon, Steve Wolf from *Sports Illustrated* was interviewing me — I was so proud that the sports world was paying attention to our athletic show — when he received a page. He went in to our company office to receive information on the wire. Nancy Kerrigan had been hit in the leg by an unknown assailant in Detroit at Nationals. The world would soon learn that the beautiful sport of figure skating was not without its ugly side, and that its ice princesses had to be tough.

Unable to skate, I watched the show that night, for the first time, as an audience member. My understudy, Delene MacKenzie, performed the role of Cinderella and she was breathtaking. We had hired her because she was a beautiful skater, but then she stunned us all with the emotion she brought to the character. She had earned the part, and I was so proud to see her skate it. She brought tears of enjoyment to my eyes. Sitting there in the audience with my broken rib, I realized I had achieved my dream. I had created a show that could go on without me. It didn't need my name recognition: It stood on its own merits and people wanted to see it.

In the morning, sweet five-year-old Alex ran a bath for me and even helped pack our suitcase. She knew I was in pain and she wanted to help. Then we drove to my parents' house in Greenwich so that I could recuperate. There was a definite pattern to my life. When things got tough, I could always count on my parents.

Family Channel assumed I would stay on

with the show after they bought it and were willing to pay me handsomely. But they told me my husband had to go. They never told me why they wanted him out of there. Ken was very insulted, as was I. I backed up my husband and told Family Channel that if he wasn't included, then I could not do it. I felt that if I stayed on, I would be selling my soul.

Another kind of devil was nipping at my heels. A *National Enquirer* reporter approached me in the lobby of our hotel in Los Angeles. He asked me if I wanted to see the pictures he had of Ken and our friend, Maria, holding and kissing each other. After Check-up Express had disbanded, she had stayed in our lives when she introduced us to her cousin, Claudia. Claudia came to work for us, helping to take care of Alex. The reporter didn't know that both Ken and Maria had previously approached me separately and warned me that such a photo existed and that it had gotten in the hands of the *National Enquirer*. Ken and Maria both told me the same story. They said Maria's former boss had sent the photo to the *National Enquirer* to get back at Maria. They were insistent that Ken was hugging Maria to congratulate her on her wedding engagement. She was marrying a detective, and the former boss was jealous. The reporter wanted me to comment on the photo and threatened to publish it.

"What do you think of this?" He tried to show me the photo, but I refused to look at it.

"I don't appreciate you doing this. It's not true." I walked on as fast as I could.

The deal was finally finished, and I skated my last show. I had come to the conclusion that I couldn't do this anymore. I made an announcement to the cast and crew. I told them we had sold the show to the Family Channel and wished them all well.

I was never reimbursed for the hundreds of thousands of dollars I put into the company, but at that point I didn't fight it because all I wanted was to be a mother to Alex.

12
DIVORCE, DOROTHY STYLE

The skating world received the truth about John Curry. He was dying of AIDS. I was devastated, and frightened he would die without ever knowing how I felt about him. So many AIDS victims were being prevented from discussing their disease, and we didn't know they were dying. The man who was responsible for my wedge haircut, Suga, had just died and it was rumored he had succumbed to AIDS. He was one of my best friends, but he never told me he was sick. I was heartbroken. He lived in a culture and a time period that had silenced his truth. I was lucky to have this wonderful person enter my life when he had cut my hair on an emergency basis the night before I'd left for the Olympics. For the next fourteen years, he was the only person to cut my hair. He was a master. He died on September 14, 1990. I never had the chance to say good-bye. I wasn't going to let that happen with John

Curry. I wrote John a letter telling him what a great man I thought he was, what he meant to me, and meant to the world of skating. I was proud that soon after that he began to speak openly about his disease. He died in 1994. An era in figure skating had come to a close.

Meanwhile, an era in my personal life was just beginning. Ken's mother, who was completely deaf, had been living with us for almost two years because Ken felt it was safer for her than living alone. I liked her. She was a straight-shooter who was easy to have in the house because she was independent. She had to go into the hospital for gall bladder surgery. The next day, Ken went up to Portland on a matter involving one of the Ice Capades rinks we managed. Our managerial contracts with rinks were still active. I was left taking care of his mother post-surgery.

Then I received the phone call that would change my life forever. It was from the manager of the Portland rink, James, a young man I trusted and had hired to run the ice rink.

"Dorothy, what is your husband doing standing in the middle of the ice holding hands and kissing a young girl?"

"W-w-hat?" I stammered.

I didn't want to believe him, of course, but

James was someone I could rely on. He wouldn't make up such a thing. I hung up and talked to my assistant, Cindi.

"Cindi, tell me what you know."

Her eyes filled with anguish.

"It is true. Ken and Kristin are having an affair."

Kristin was my double in *Cinderella*. The irony was that I had been the one who had fought to hire Kristin when others on our creative team didn't think she was a strong enough skater, although she was beautiful.

Cindi went on, "I didn't want to have to tell you. I was hoping the *National Enquirer* episode would scare him off."

"If you knew, if you saw it, then others did?" I asked, wondering how I could have been so blind.

"There's more. But Maria will have to tell you."

"Maria?"

"Your neighbor told me she heard Ken and Maria in your Jacuzzi together when you were out of town."

My breath stopped. Maria? My friend?

"People in the show were afraid to tell you. Because there were only rumors. Nobody had any evidence."

I called Maria and asked her to come over. When she came in, I was surprised at how open she was and how ready she was to tell the truth. But she had no reason to hold back. By this time she was married to a wonderful man and had gone on with her life.

Maria said her affair with Ken had begun when I was six months pregnant.

I quickly thought back to what Dean had warned me about Ken. He had been right!

Maria had been in love with Ken, but he had said he never would leave me because I was "too good an opportunity" for him.

She also answered the mysterious question of why Claudia, the nanny she had introduced us to, had suddenly left us. Claudia's boyfriend had picked her up in the middle of the night and I'd never known why she'd left. I remembered feeling very angry that she had left so suddenly and without a word of explanation. Maria explained that Claudia had caught Ken and Maria together. Since Maria was her cousin, she hadn't wanted to come between family and her employer, and the only solution had been to leave as soon as possible. Maria had come to Arizona to fill in for Claudia. She'd been angry with Ken because he was having an affair with Kristin. She'd stopped seeing him at that point.

It seemed like everyone but me knew my husband had been having affairs for six years while I'd stupidly believed I had a blissful home life with an attentive, loving husband! He had gotten so comfortable with his affairs that he had flown Kristin from her home in Vancouver and was cavorting with her right in front of the rink manager. It was plane fare I had paid for: It was on my credit card.

I called Ken. "I think you'd better come home."

He knew it was serious. "I'll be right there."

When he came home, I confronted him. I was still hoping that somehow it wasn't true. But, of course, it was.

He fully admitted to everything I had discovered. He didn't seem sincerely apologetic for what he had done. But he did seem sincere when he said he would never do it again.

I faced further humiliation when the *National Enquirer* called for my comment. They ran an article about Ken cheating on me with "a young Dorothy Hamill." Kristin had been hired to be my double because when she was in costume, she looked like me under the spotlights.

Soon I received a call from Kristin's mother chastising me, "Can't you control your husband? My daughter's so young."

I was taken so much by surprise, I didn't know what to say. No, I couldn't control him just as she couldn't control her daughter. But it wasn't about control. I hadn't known! Even if I *had* known, how does a wife control it? It was an illogical assumption from a mother clearly upset that her daughter was having an affair with a married man three times her age.

I tried to imagine when Ken had had time for his affairs. He'd always seemed so busy with Check-up Express and after that, running Ice Capades. Then it dawned on me. Every time he said he had a meeting, or a golf date, or was going to work out at the gym, he'd been cavorting, first with Maria and then Kristin. There could have been more affairs for all I knew, but no one else was coming forward. I had become a cliché: "The wife is the last to know."

My first instinct was not to divorce him. My primary goal was to try and work it out for the sake of our daughter. Ken and I began seeing a psychologist who specialized in marriage counseling. Ken hadn't gotten a job, and he didn't seem to be concerned about it. I seemed to be the one agonizing over the big questions. What was I going to do with my life? How were we going to earn a living? I'd break down crying several times a day. It didn't matter what I was doing or where I was. The tears would flow. I'd be out to lunch, and I'd suddenly start crying uncontrollably. Whether I was with someone else or by myself, I'd burst into tears.

I had to protect my daughter from this ugliness. I enrolled her in kindergarten at home in Indian Wells. The time spent in the Arizona kindergarten had not been very long. Ken said, "She doesn't need to be in kindergarten. She knows all that stuff." But Alex needed some structure.

Ken's mother came home from the hospital. Because of her deafness, she couldn't hear our arguing, but even without sound, she could certainly feel the tension. To answer her inquisitiveness, I showed her the article from the *National Enquirer*. That told the whole story. She shook her head in disbelief, trying to be very understanding toward me, but I still got the feeling she felt her son could do no wrong.

I visited my OB/GYN. He saw that I was traumatized and prescribed Paxil to help me. I started taking it. It would be a while before I would feel its positive effects. My crying jags were upsetting the household. Ken's children, Jennifer and Daniel, came for their visit, and I asked Ken to talk to all the children about my behavior so they wouldn't think I was going crazy. I thought he was going to find some appropriate way to communicate with them, but I could not have possibly predicted what he did. He bluntly told them he had been having an affair. The children were much too young to hear this. I began to see the sparkle disappear from Alex's eyes. Her whole world was crumbling. The life she thought was so happy was not what she thought it was. I was incapable of reaching out to her to stop her pain. I was having suicidal thoughts, giving great thought to driving my car into a wall and ending it all. I tried so hard not to have those thoughts, but it was difficult. What stopped me from going through with it were, of course, thoughts of Alex. I could never do that to her.

Meanwhile, Ken was trying to turn on his charm. We would work it out, he insisted. He also said we should have another baby. I knew I was shrouded in anguish, but I managed some rational thought, realizing that that suggestion didn't make any sense. He had started having an affair when I was pregnant. How could he think I would trust him to want to get pregnant again with him? He was only convincing when he said he would work with the marriage counselor. I believed marriage was about working it out and doing everything possible to make things better for one's children.

Looking over our unhealthy financial situation, it became clear that Ken had to get a job. He said that practicing medicine was boring to him and still, despite so many failures, thought of himself as an entrepreneur. His father had been successful in many businesses, and he preferred his father's lifestyle.

"As long as you're with Ken, you're a sinking ship," Steve, my trusted accountant, said to me.

"Can't you contribute something, Ken?" I would plead with him. But I'd be thinking, We're in this sinking ship together, Ken. Pick up an oar and start rowing.

I couldn't understand what he thought was going to happen.

Soon after that, Steve quit. "I can't work with Ken anymore," he stated.

We were to see the counselor both alone as well as together. Ken stopped going on his own. I went on a regular basis. It hit me hard that we were not fighting the good fight together. I was in this alone. It was falling on my shoulders only. Almost as awful, it was my name out there getting stung. I had lost several lucrative endorsements because of the debacle with his affair.

Then I realized I had lost something more precious.

I had lost my love of skating.

We had no money, and the only way we could become solvent was by my skating. But I didn't care if I ever skated again. I had lost my joy of skating while trying to run Ice Capades and having to worry about snow machines instead of concentrating on skating.

The Paxil could not change my life's situation, but it did improve my ability to deal with it. It became obvious. After much thought and loads of counseling, I felt the best thing for Alex and me would be if I filed for divorce — but I still hoped Ken would change.

Friends had hoped they could help us stay together. Our dear neighbor, Stuart, tried to advise Ken on what he should do to fix our marriage. It was then, when I had to admit it to Stuart, that I admitted it to myself. It was more complicated than anyone was imagining. There was no trust. Personal or financial.

We had signed a postnuptial agreement, which stated that what had been mine before we were married would remain mine. Lawyers had pressured me to have one drawn up. We put it in the safe with other important documents, like our birth certificates, proclaiming, "We'll tear it up in fifteen years while drinking a glass of champagne."

But when I went looking, our copy was not in the safe. It had disappeared. I asked Ken where our copy was, and he insisted that he didn't know what I was talking about.

But the postnup would not have made a difference. What I'd had before I was married was all gone.

I filed Chapter 11 bankruptcy and reorganization. I went to court feeling shame and embarrassment, so emotionally fragile I don't know how I got through it. Margaret, Ken's ex-wife and the mother of their two children, began leaving desperate messages for Ken. Evidently, he was not answering her calls, so I finally picked up the phone and talked to her. She was panicked and wondered what had happened to her alimony and child support payments. She was strapped financially and dependent on these payments. It came as a blow to her that I had been the one making her payments for all those years. She was a lovely woman who was a wonderful mother to her children, and I had always held her in the highest regard. We genuinely liked each other and had gotten along well the few times we had spent together. I hadn't known what I was getting into with Ken's situation when I married him and had to make those payments for eight years. Now I had to give it to her straight.

"I've filed for bankruptcy."

"What am I supposed to do?" she asked.

"I'm sorry for you, but I can't do it anymore."

My only responsibility was to Alex. It was the summer of 1996: Palm Springs was frightfully hot. My mood always suffered in the summer heat and I had to get out of there. I took Alex and flew back East. My place of refuge was, once again, my parents'. I ended up spending the summer on their couch. I slumped down on it and wasn't able to get up. I managed to enroll Alex in a dance camp and she had her cousin, Becky, to play with, but other than doing that, I was a basket case. I was sad, confused, disappointed, angry — every emotion at once. I curled up in a fetal position. I didn't want to do anything.

I was in the depth of a depression. I had hit rock bottom. I kept up with the Paxil, but I was supplementing it with glasses of white wine. Not a good idea. But I had run out of good ideas. To add to my misery, I started smoking as a complement to my glasses of wine.

Despite the difficulties I'd had with my parents, there was no place else I felt I could be at this time. I was like another Dorothy, one much more celebrated than I, when she says in *The Wizard of Oz,* "There's no place like home."

My mother never said, "I told you so," although she could have. She was very sad for me and hated to see Alex hurting so much. During this time, she was never opinionated nor did she form judgments. Instead, she was incredible, always supportive, and she helped me get through my days. I tried to explain to my parents what had happened with the business of Ice Capades, but it was hard for them to understand. Still, I learned I could count on my family no matter what — at least, when the chips were down and we weren't counting the almighty dollar.

I desperately wanted the divorce to be finalized so that I could move on, but it dragged on and on, and it was dragging me down. Ken kept fighting to get more money out of me, but there was none to get. He thought he was entitled to live at the same level of lifestyle "to which he had become accustomed." But I wasn't even living at that level anymore, so how could he expect to? I was on my parents' couch. I knew I had to sell the Indian Wells home and move to a less expensive home. Ken wrongly assumed that I intended to sue the Family Channel for the money I had put into Ice Capades to keep it afloat while the deal was finished. But I had no intention of battling the behemoth Pat Robertson empire. I could barely get off of the couch!

Then the worst possible thing happened. Ken fought me for sole custody of Alex. He had finally gotten a job. It was in Stockton, California, and he moved up there with his mother. He argued that he could give Alex a nice, stable home life, whereas I always had to travel for my work. I found it hard to believe that a man who had forsaken his first two children, ignoring their needs when they came to visit us, and committing adultery not once but twice when his wives were pregnant, suddenly cared for his little daughter so much. Turns out, I was naïve about this motive as well. My lawyers explained to me that I would have to pay him more if he won primary physical custody. They said that after he won custody, he could quit working and I would have to pay him even more. I would have to work while Ken raised her.

I had to get off of that darn couch!

No one was going to raise my daughter but me!

Slowly, the fog began to lift.

My source of strength was Alex. I knew that I had to start over to give her a life. I thought logically about where I could live. Where did it make sense? I knew that I wanted to come back East to be near my family. I would have loved to live in Greenwich again, but now I couldn't afford it. I had sold my home there when Ken and I had moved to Indian Wells. Besides, the skating rink situation would have been more complicated for me there. My choreographer, Tim Murphy, had become my best friend, and he lived in Baltimore, where he had a nice set-up with a rink. He showed me an area of homes in Baltimore that I fell in love with. I had other friends in Baltimore who began to tell me about some of the schools there and which ones would be good for Alex. One of the schools had an opening, and she interviewed there. They said she could start in the fall. Luckily, friends of mine owned a home near the school and let me rent it. Although I wasn't ready to buy a home yet, this house became the place where I was able to get my life back together.

I went back to California with Alex and showed the judge a picture of the rental house and a picture of Alex's school. I pleaded with the court not to use my career against me. If they persisted, if it meant keeping my daughter, I would quit the road. I explained that I could get a job teaching in the Baltimore area. I would be making far less for her future, but I would do whatever was necessary. I told the judge that I didn't know if I still had a career. There was no way of knowing if I was ever going to be hired to perform again. Not only had the Ice Capades debacle hurt me, but audiences wanted to see the Tonyas and the Nancys of the skating world, not a soon-to-be-forty "America's ex-Sweetheart."

The court-appointed psychologist privately interviewed Alex. He also called in my assistant, Cindi, to give testimony, and then he called in Maria. She had betrayed me in the worst way, but she tried to make it up to me with her frank testimony. When the female judge realized what Ken had done to ruin our family life, she awarded me custody despite Ken's machinations. Ken would get Alex every other Christmas and half of every summer. I was ordered to pay her way to California for these visits, and I would have to pay him child support, even though she was with me throughout the year. But it meant Alex and I were free to move to Baltimore and start anew.

13
THE RACEHORSE BACK AT THE STARTING GATE

"We're poor."

Alex was sitting at the kitchen table, looking very worried.

"Why do you say that, honey?"

"Courtney said that about us."

"We're not poor. We're very lucky to have each other."

Parents at her school had obviously been talking about my bankruptcy, and some of their children had overheard it. It had gotten back to Alex, who was now in the third grade.

"Millie says you're retired."

"Do you know what 'retired' means?"

"No."

"It means I've stopped working."

"But you're not stopped working, are you?"

"No. So you know I'm not retired."

Truthfully, I hadn't been on the ice for more than eight months. Even with my pregnancy, this was the longest hiatus I'd had in my three decades of skating. My muscles had turned to mush. My legal fees had mounted during the excruciatingly long divorce and I detested owing money, but I was so unsure of myself that I refused offers of performing. A producer created a new competition, Legends on Ice, and called me, offering a substantial appearance fee. I had never done anything else in my life to earn a living besides performing. It took me a long time to convince myself that I could do it, and I finally called back, committing myself to the rigors of the road and the demands of performing once again. The problem was, I only had two weeks to get myself in shape while Alex was in school. Obviously, I had not been taking care of myself. I had been eating poorly and hadn't done any physical activity, unable to even start on a walking regimen. I don't know what made me think I could do it, I only knew I *had* to do it.

When I was little, I skated on public sessions, and here I was at forty seeking public ice time again. I bought my ticket and managed to get myself out there, marveling at how unsteady I was. That first day, I only stroked around the ice — no way was I ready for jumps and spins. I remembered from my Gus Lussi training that if skaters were off the ice for as short a time as a week, we were to get back into it slowly, concentrating on our edges. But I couldn't feel my edges. It's typical, when a skater is unprepared, tired, or nervous, to scratch on the toepicks and not be in control. Here I was, after three decades of skating, scratching on my toes. I didn't feel I had the strength to center on my blades. I focused on my knees, bending down into the ice instead of skating on top of it.

Then came the moment I had been hoping, waiting, and praying for. Being out there felt *good.* I gradually got that good old feeling of freedom and peacefulness that had sustained me throughout good times and bad. Could I keep it up? Skating had always been there for me. It had been my savior many times before. Could I count on it now? I could only last for an hour at that first session, but it gave me hope.

I knew I wanted to find my love of skating again. I couldn't let the buy-out of Ice Capades or an ugly divorce ruin what was my passion. I was rusty, but I had a purpose — to prove to myself that life hadn't beaten me down.

It was my love of music that sustained me through this difficult time. I could always count on music to lift my mood. Just as I did when I was young and felt so passionate about a song like "Edelweiss," I found I could still go into a rink, put on a piece of music, and be completely inspired by it. It was as if the music itself compelled me to move. It has always been that way, and I pray that it always will be. I also realized music had the innate ability to make me forget about my problems. And, boy, if there was ever a time when I needed to de-stress, it was now. When I was younger, I thought it was "all about the dress": Now, I was sure it was "all about the music." Tim Murphy and I choreographed a number to Louis Armstrong's "What a Wonderful World." I wanted to believe that for me, it could be wonderful again.

I was forty and dreadfully nervous when I stepped in front of an audience again. I managed to smile my way through a two-minute, forty-second routine, about the length of a juvenile ladies program. It was the audience who carried me through it. I was more grateful for them than I had ever been. But they could not possibly be expected to carry me through what happened next.

Thursday. September 19, 1998. It was Alex's tenth birthday. We were settling into the Baltimore house. While kneeling to unpack an unassembled storage unit, four heavy doors fell like an avalanche directly onto my head. I ended up in the ER getting stitches to close a gash in my head. An examination revealed a bruised collarbone, and the doctor wanted more tests because he suspected something worse. But I had to get on the plane the next day to Little Rock for another Legends on Ice.

It was a small rink, and I traveled on one of my flying camels, nearly sending me into the boards. I never had good depth perception on the ice and could never see that well out there. But now it seemed worse. I couldn't count on my neck turning because it was so stiff. I let my adrenaline take over, as it had for me so many times. Somehow, I won the competition on both Saturday and Sunday. I have found that champions don't allow themselves to have a sick day. No matter how bad a champion feels when he or she gets out on the ice, they fight through it and go on with the show. The mind takes over, and before you know it, it's over.

But the mind and adrenaline can't conquer a herniated disk. The doors falling on my head had caused compression in my neck. My fingers became numb. The pain was so severe I couldn't sleep. I'd sit at the end of the bed in the hotel room on the road, crying in pain, knowing that the next day I had to make myself skate or I wasn't getting paid. Not getting paid meant I was frittering away precious time from my precious daughter and wasting away in hotel rooms. I was aching all over. In the morning, I'd barely be able to shuffle to the bathroom. I was expecting my body to perform at a high level, yet my body never had a chance to heal. Even the long bus rides on tour were intolerable, as sitting so long caused my body to seize up on me. Finally, doctors diagnosed me with osteoarthritis, what I thought was an old-lady disease — something I certainly never expected to have at forty. It was most severe in my neck, but I also had it in my hips and in my lower back. A doctor told me that I didn't get this from skating. It was hereditary. I remembered looking at pictures my grandmother Jonsie where she was wearing a cervical collar. I had to have shots in my cervical spine and I started megadosing on Advil. I was determined to piece myself together and soldier on, both on and off the ice.

I was still a single parent, no matter where I was in my own life. I had to take on the roles of dual parenting, to juggle Alex's needs, which were the priority. It wasn't easier when I was home and off the road. We were both wading through the aftershocks of the divorce, and I wanted to hold her little hand the whole way. I kept the lines of communication open between us by acknowledging her feelings. I was able to teach her that it was not her fault. She could understand that her mother was not perfect and that I made mistakes. I was a great believer in seeking help from a psychologist, and I found a good one for Alex. I wanted to make sure I wasn't overlooking anything important to her. The pressure of doing it all, combining a career with cooking, the laundry, carpooling, after-school sports, homework, and on and on was dragging me down.

I was beginning to appreciate what my mother had done for me more and more. Here I was, a single working mom, and I was getting a clearer picture of what my mother had had to do raising me to be a champion, all the sacrifices she'd had to make and how difficult it must have been for her to get through the day. There were so many moments throughout my day that it would hit me hard: My parents had done an amazing job of raising us! Despite their problems and limitations, they did their best. Maybe these little epiphanies were sweeping over me so much more powerfully because I was back on the East Coast raising a child, where my own childhood memories, pre-skating, were so vivid. I found myself determined to take Alex on the same educational trips my parents had done. I drove her to Williamsburg. On the way, we passed a sign for the Luray Caverns, and I was overwhelmed with emotion. It was here that I had learned of stalagmites and stalactites at the age of six. We'd taken that trip because Sandy had expressed an interest, reminding me of my parents' desire to fulfill the potential of all their children.

These recurring thoughts made me want to take Alex to see her grandparents as often as I could. Deep down, I was realizing that they were wonderful people and I wanted her to know that.

One of these family weekends was Labor Day, 1998. Dad had not been feeling well and had just gone to the doctor for tests. We received a call from Sandy, who was now a wonderful, caring doctor. Now that we were middle-aged, my siblings and I had forged much closer bonds than those we had while growing up. Our childhoods, spent so much apart from one another, were exactly what was bonding us as adults because of what we had in common — our set of unique parents.

"Dad's not doing well," Sandy said, sadly.

"What do you mean?"

"He has cancer."

"How can that be?" I was in shock.

"Dorothy, he probably only has a few weeks to live."

The family all came together for that Labor Day weekend. I was supposed to be rehearsing for a TV show, and I canceled it. We had a beautiful few days with Dad. At least it was for us. Dad had a blood transfusion, and he seemed frail and tired. He was on large doses of morphine. Still, it was impossible to believe that he was a dying man and that this would be the last time I would see him alive.

I had to get Alex back home and in school. I quickly made arrangements to fly up again to see him. But too soon, I got another call from Sandy.

"Dad has passed." He was calling from my parrent's home.

"No." I was in disbelief. This was too quick. We'd had little warning. I really believed I would see him one more time before he died.

"He died peacefully. He wasn't in any pain."

"I'm still coming anyway." I'd made up my mind.

"You are?"

"Yes. I have to see him."

"Okay. We'll keep him," he said sweetly,

meaning they would keep him in his bedroom until I arrived.

There were so many people I loved who had died, and I'd never had the chance to find closure with them. I never got a chance to say good-bye to Dean. I still dreamed of him, feeling his presence, trying to find closure and never getting it. Now I was getting on that plane to Connecticut to see my dad. I knew he was at peace and making merry music in heaven, but I still was seeking closure with him.

When I walked into his room, I hugged him and realized in just a few short hours, he had already grown so cold. His beloved dog Puffy was still by his side. I told my beautiful father that I loved him and I thanked him for being such a great father to me. I was truly grateful for all he had done for me, and I hoped I had made him proud all throughout my life. He had given me so much: a love of music and a passion to express it in my skating. He had supported my skating wholeheartedly and never once hinted that I should stop, even when things got so impossibly tough to continue. He had taught me to openly express my love with others by being ready with a hug and the simple words, "I love you." He didn't say it often, but he did say it.

I thought things would change with my mother after my father's death. But they didn't. I thought we would grow closer. But we didn't. I thought maybe she would become the parent who warmly said, "I love you." But she didn't. As Alex once said about her grandma, "She's just not a warm and fuzzy person." The few times Mom ever expressed an "I love you," it hung stiffly in the air, and it was impossible to genuinely feel its intent. I remember my grandfather Bill, my mom's father, as being all about hugs and tenderness. So I couldn't figure out how my mom got left out.

But I didn't have a moment to try to figure this out. I had to worry about bringing home a paycheck to put food on the table and a roof over my daughter's head. I had gotten a call from Tom Collins, the premier producer of Champions on Ice, the show that tours with world and Olympic champions, like Michelle Kwan and Elvis Stojko. He wanted me to join them. He had actually called a year earlier to ask me, but I had been honest and told him I wasn't up to it. Now, things were different. The FDA had approved a new drug for osteoarthritis, and my doctor suggested that I try it. He said that I was a perfect candidate for it because of my history of bleeding ulcers. The Advil was tough on my stomach lining, and this new drug, Vioxx, would be easier on it. I started feeling good from the medicine, and from my excruciating but diligent physical therapy. I went to my buddy Tim Murphy, and he choreographed two wonderful numbers for me.

Next, I had to arrange my schedule so that I was never away from Alex for more than five days at a time. This demand had been decreed by court order, but I also didn't want to be away from her. Luckily, Tom Collins was a devoted parent himself, and he understood my dilemma. He put skaters up in first-class hotels in major cities, which would then become our satellite from which to travel to other towns. We'd travel two hours to one city, then come back to spend the night in the same place, and the next night travel two hours to another venue. It was a workable situation for me. I could either easily get home or Alex would come on the road with me. She never once complained about her mother being away, but I could hear it in her voice. She knew how hard it was on me, and she didn't want to worry me. She once confided to her school counselor about her loneliness, but told the advisor, "Don't tell my mom. I don't want her to worry." I felt tremendous guilt associated with my travel, but fortunately, these tours were for short seasons at a time. They afforded me the opportunity to be home with her full-time the rest of the year. When she was on the road with me, the other skaters, the wardrobe people, the lighting crew, and others were always so good to her. We were together a lot, so it was easy to be open and honest with her about my feelings.

It was so important to me that I have a completely different relationship with my daughter than I had had with my mother. I'd hated how Mom wasn't open with me and how she'd made it so difficult to talk to her about my problems and how I was feeling. My mom was a yeller and I am not, because I didn't want to emulate her. I thought if I was honest with Alex, she would turn around and learn to be open with me — especially in the tumultuous teenage years that were fast approaching. My parents didn't teach me how to communicate my feelings, and, darn it all, I was going to make sure Alex could. I would always explain to Alex how I felt as a kid, thinking that I was helping her to express her own feelings. Thankfully, she became open with me, but this parent-child thing is not a perfect science. Since I was not a yeller, when I did let it all out and sounded like my mother, Alex was devastated. I'd apologize and try to pump her up with praise. Maybe this was bottled-up praise my mother never gave me — and sometimes I went overboard.

Professionally, I was feeling more capable on tour. I was traveling and skating with champions half my age. I felt like a dinosaur compared to them, but it didn't stop me from wanting to perform. It was very thrilling to skate with the top world-class skaters of the day. Physically and mentally, I did not find the tour as demanding as my previous stint of touring had been. Tom Collins made it fun, and getting a regular paycheck, without having to worry about ticket sales and promotion as I had sweating it out as an owner of Ice Capades, was nice. Obviously, I couldn't keep up with the other skaters' triples, but I suppose I was on the tour for another reason. There were people in the audience who were my age — basically, the adults purchasing the tickets. Their children probably thought I was some granny out there. But no one ever made me feel old. I always asked for more warm-up time, because it took me so much longer to get ready for a performance. We'd practice four hours ahead of each show, and the warm-up would be split evenly among men, women, and pairs. I'd always ask for more time on the other sessions, and the other skaters were always very accommodating. What took others a half hour to do took me three times as long. There would have to be time for interviews, and after the exhibitions, there'd be lines of people waiting for autographs before the ride back to the hotel. Still, it wasn't exhausting. It was great not to have all the other responsibilities. I just went out and did my numbers for four minutes, and then I was done.

Vioxx was making it possible for me to skate alongside these kids half my age. I had been offered many endorsements over the years, far more than I ever took, but I had never accepted an offer unless I totally believed in the product. I always saw endorsements as a bonus and knew not to count on them because it was so difficult to find the right fit.

I stayed on the Vioxx while I was on tour, but when I went off the tour and was home, I stopped taking it because I was feeling so wonderful, and since I wasn't in training for performances, I thought I didn't need it. But soon the same aching feeling swept over me again. My local doctor told me to go back on the Vioxx. Merck offered me an endorsement for the drug, and because I believed in the medicine so much, I went off to shoot my first commercial.

Tim Murphy and another John Curry colleague, Nathan Birch, had started their own company, The Next Ice Age, years earlier, and put together a ten-year anniversary celebration of their company to the music of Steely Dan. We were to open at the Kennedy Center in Washington, DC, on September 14, 2001. We were on our way to rehearsal when the planes hit the World Trade Center and the Pentagon, and were paralyzed with shock and grief with the rest of the nation — and the world. We were shut down, emotionally and physically, and we assumed that the show would be shut down as well. The cast and crew were ready to pack up and go home when the call came from the Kennedy Center. They encouraged us to go on with the show. They wanted us to do it more than ever. We didn't understand why, and we certainly didn't know *how* we would do it. But we had paying customers, so we went ahead as planned. We felt foolish for continuing. Our show seemed so insignificant and unimportant in the shadow of September 11.

"This is crazy," we said. "Why are we doing this?"

As soon as we got out on the ice and the lights went up, we understood why we were there. The house was full, and it became clear why people had come. Every face was filled with sadness, and they desperately needed escape, a diversion from the hell of 9/11. For that moment, we were more than just skaters putting on a show. Although we were a slight, pleasant distraction, we were also a leap into their past, before the unbearable pain had filled their hearts. They had bought the tickets to our show when they felt happy, and they thought that by seeing us they could feel that again. Sometimes I say, "I'm just a skater," but that night I felt that I, along with all the other skaters, meant more to those people than I had at any other performance.

14
GOLDEN SNOWFLAKES

Merck pulled my commercials in 2003, and they began airing new commercials with noncelebrities. The medication was allowing me to keep performing on the ice and off. I knew that the company had included a warning label in the package inserts about adverse reactions, and I wanted to make sure I was still okay to take it, so I consulted my physician. I was assured that because I had no history of cardiovascular ailments, and since I was taking it specifically for my osteoarthritis, I was not a high-risk patient and it would be all right to stay on it.

Then Merck announced a voluntary worldwide withdrawal of Vioxx from the marketplace. Knowing I could no longer get it, I starting saving the pills to take only on my really bad days. Taken regularly, and letting the drug have a cumulative effect, the Vioxx worked well for me. But taking it on and off, it didn't. When the pills ran out, it was back to over-the-counter medication. Five years earlier, before I had been diagnosed with osteoarthritis but was beginning to feel the achiness associated with the disease, I had tried other medications, but these hadn't worked either.

I was so desperate I asked Ken what I should do. He was back working in sports medicine, and I wanted to believe he could help me.

Thankfully, he did.

When Alex and I moved to Baltimore, I had kept my contact with Ken to a minimum to avoid confrontation. Our phone conversations were brief and limited to facts only, to discuss Alex's travel arrangements to California for her visitations with Ken. I stayed off the phone calls between Alex and her father. It was their special time together, and it was not my place to get in the middle of it. Despite what had happened between Ken and me, it was important to me that Alex have a healthy relationship with her father. For the first few years after our separation, it was very tense with Ken, but as time went by, it got easier.

So a couple years ago, after too much time had been wasted, unable to find something that took the pain away, I was at my wit's end, and I asked Ken what I should do.

"There has to be something out on the market for osteoarthritis sufferers. There are millions of us."

He said that he would research it. And he soon got back to me, suggesting another anti-inflammatory.

"See if it makes a difference."

I was skeptical but willing to try it.

I've been on it for a year and a half, and so far, so good. And I have Ken to thank. I can go on skating, and I'm still performing at fifty years old. One of my latest ventures was teaming up with Davis Gaines, the phenomenal singer who performed the title role in *Phantom of the Opera* over two thousand times on Broadway, to tour in Willy Bietak's Broadway on Ice, a revue of over forty Tony Award–winning songs, from "All That Jazz" to Gershwin's "Rhapsody in Blue." Willy created this show in the 1980s, and it has had a rotating cast of skating and musical guest stars from Nancy Kerrigan to Rudy Galindo. The innovative Sarah Kawahara choreographed and directed it. Willy Bietak has been on the cutting edge of ice rink technology by setting up ice surfaces in theaters, theme parks, and television studios, on movie sets, cruise lines, and in conventions and stadiums, thus bringing figure skating closer to the public by taking it out of the conventional arena and into previously unimaginable places. I enjoy skating in a theater setting because it allows more intimacy with the audience, and the magical bonus was skating to Davis Gaines's legendary voice.

It is a show that my mother particularly likes because of the musical selections. I am so happy that, for many years now, she has been able to enjoy watching me skate and not anguish over whether I'm going to make a mistake. It took me many years to appreciate all that she did for me; incredibly, the first step was when I became a mother myself. The years spent raising my daughter as a single mom paralleled, to some extent, the circumstances my mother had. Being away from my dad, she had to do all the work herself and make all the difficult decisions on her own. As my own daughter nears the age at which I won the Olympics, I seem to appreciate my mother more each day. What makes her sacrifice all the more compelling to me is that she did it while afflicted with an untreated and undiagnosed mood disorder.

Mom is still a part of the generation that never spoke of such disorders, so she can't help but remain silent about it. She has yet to discuss with me the chemical imbalance she suffers. But we did come close once. We were sitting in her kitchen when a pill she was taking dropped to the floor. I picked it up for her and could tell what it was, a common antidepressant.

I gave it to her, saying, "Oh, you're taking Zoloft."

She nodded and swallowed it. Tears sprang to my eyes. My mother had sought help! It was the first time I knew that she had. I was truly happy for her.

My brother, a brilliant physician and now the cornerstone of our family, believes she may have something called dysthymic disorder. It is characterized by periods of habitual gloominess, pessimism, hypercriticism, and a preoccupation with inadequacy and negative events. It is felt that perhaps she had the disorder as a very young girl: My grandfather had taken her to doctors to figure out why she was never happy or satisfied. Since this was in the 1930s, there were no answers except counterproductive ones.

But it has also since been discovered that dysthymic persons are especially adept in work that involves dedication and painstaking attention to detail. Although her hypercriticism and negativity sometimes made our family life a nightmare, these other manifestations certainly were helpful in dealing with the skating world. Maybe this is what made it possible for her to maneuver through the mess in a way other mothers wouldn't dare, enabling her to stand up to the male hierarchy that dominated the sport. Years later, I would learn that she was very much admired and well liked by many parents, especially other mothers and many skaters who looked up to her as a leader. Some friends from the Ice Capades days, believed that I learned my leadership skills from my mother. My mother is what many call a "tough old bird." Perhaps these characteristics have helped her to be a cancer survivor for over twenty years now. She has so much goodness in her that it is heartbreaking to see her down. The cycles of a mood disorder can be very erratic, way up one day, way down the next. Despite these moods, she has an inherent goodness in her. It was this goodness in her that made her give me her last five dollars to get something to eat in Denver, and it was her goodness that took in the schizophrenic young man hiding in her garage and fed him after I had won the Olympics. There is a willingness in her to see the best in everybody.

But she still doesn't give me a reason why she was not in the arena to watch me win the Olympics. She says, "There was nothing I could do for you then," trying to explain why she was back at the hotel, even though she was not expected to do anything for me at that point. Because of her strength as a mother, she still felt she was supposed to. I believe that she had some understanding of her own negativity and didn't want to bring any of it to the arena. In that way, she made the ultimate sacrifice. To her, it would have been a selfish act to come to the arena, putting her needs ahead of mine because, of course, she wanted to watch me. She feared that one of her critical glances would have spoiled my mood and affected my performance. She knew by staying back at the hotel that there was a chance that hope and optimism were carrying me through. She made so many sacrifices for me, but her ultimate sacrifice was missing the event we had both been working so hard toward. I am so relieved that she is finally getting help for a condition that prevented her from enjoying seeing her daughter win an Olympic gold medal.

I've tried to be as open as possible about my own chemical imbalance, but it has taken many years to figure out what it is. Twenty percent of women and 10 percent of men suffer from some form of depressive disorder. Most of these disorders have a genetic origin, some are environmental, and some are both. I think mine is both. The genetic aspect comes from both sides of my family, so I had little chance of escaping it. My siblings have also had to deal with the disorder, in one way or another. There is no one to blame for such a disorder, only myself if I don't learn how to deal with it. I have sought the help of many doctors, and it now seems I have seasonal affective disorder (SAD). Mine does not occur in the winter as is most common for this disorder. My debilitating symptoms occur in the summertime. I become extremely lethargic and depressed, sometimes so paralyzed I don't want to get off of the couch. My sleep is disturbed, and I find myself waking up in the middle of the night or needing to sleep at odd hours. I have an increased need for sweets and always gain weight. Most of all, I don't want to be social.

I believe my symptoms started over twenty years ago. Looking back, I think I first noticed it in the summer of 1983, when Dean left me. Every summer after that, I detected changes in my mood, but I attributed them to the reality of my work. Because skating tours, ice shows, and television production slowed down in the summer, I would always have far less work throughout those months, so obviously I would have to expend less energy anyway. I've always been much more active in the winter and always felt happier when temperatures would cool — thus I assumed it was work that kept me happy. The debilitating summer I spent on my parents' couch was certainly triggered by the breakup with Ken, but there would also be summers where everything was fine, and I'd still be so lethargic, irritable and depressed, it'd be too much trouble just to unload the dishwasher.

Science does not seem to know as much about what causes the summer SAD as they do about what causes winter SAD. I know, for me, that it is definitely the change in temperature. I don't like heat and keep our air-conditioning up so high throughout the summer my daughter thinks icicles could form on our ceiling. Relief comes when the leaves start to change color in the fall. I love October through the end of May. Just as medicine has helped my body to work, it has helped my mind to feel balanced.

Everybody has bad times. It doesn't matter how much money one has or doesn't have, it doesn't matter if someone is famous or not. What does matter is the readiness to find help when it's needed. My parents behavior was my prime example of how to deal with depression. They hid their emotions and drank alcohol to change their mood, making a bad situation worse and essentially putting gasoline on a fire. But maybe, in our case, I've been a good example to my own mother, who finally sought help.

In the best of worlds, running a family is the most difficult thing to do. Being a full-time single working mom is even harder, harder than winning the Olympics, harder than anything I've ever done. I knew how to win the Olympics, but I don't know how to win a medal for Great Single Mom. This gold medal will always elude me. I can't be good cop, bad cop, chauffeur, disciplinarian, chef, friend, support, and nag all rolled up into one person, who then is supposed to go out searching for a lover and a mate. I'm not an advocate for single parenthood, but I'm also not an advocate to stay in a rotten marriage. I never dreamed I'd be fifty years old and not have a wonderful husband and family. This has been the hardest thing for me to accept. I assumed it was the natural course of things to have a man to share life with and children whom we would both love and adore. Of course, my family life, growing up, was far from ideal, but I had no idea it was preparing me to make the poor judgments I have about people and relationships. And still do. I think about it all the time — why I have had such bad judgment — and the basis of it is that I never learned to communicate my feelings. I am open to finding the man of my dreams, but I don't want to make another mistake. I'm a work in progress.

At times, I feel overwhelmed and my depression leads me into darkness. I still have occasional suicidal thoughts when I'm at my lowest, but I know how to take action to correct my inherent chemical imbalances. For me, exercise, vitamins, and old-fashioned fortitude aren't enough. I exercise hard every single day, renting out ice time for my intense two-hour workouts, and of course, I take vitamins. I believe I have fortitude or I wouldn't have made it this far. But these are not enough. Proper diagnosis, the right medication, and therapy, exactly what my parents never had, are the tools that work for me.

Sometimes I think maybe I had this disorder as a little girl, before I started skating, and found in skating a way to make myself happy. My self-esteem was so low, I thought I was the ugliest, stupidest, most untalented, clumsiest girl I knew. But I found my niche, a place where I could deal with those demons. It was serendipitous that, in these cold places, and on these frozen surfaces, I found something I loved and learned a way to make a living at it. Did I find skating or did it find me? It makes me believe that if it happened to me, it can happen to anyone. All it took was hard work and not giving up. And, *most of all,* a mother who sacrificed her life because she believed in me. The problem was, I didn't know she believed in me. Not until now. Not until I learned of her disorder.

I so much wanted my mother to know how much I appreciated all that she did. Believe it or not, she still berates herself for decisions she made about my skating. For instance, she still questions her decision to send me alone to Lake Placid that first summer. But I don't question it at all: I see that time period as a great period of growth for me. My sister has always pointed out to her that her decisions must have been the right ones because the end result was Olympic gold, but it has been impossible for Mom to see it that way. I had to let her know that I thought everything she did was right, and I didn't want to wait until she was on her deathbed to tell her so. She is now eighty years old.

Although words are hard to come by in our family, and so much is left unspoken, I had my chance at a recent family reunion.

My brother and sister were there, and we joked, "How can this be a Hamill reunion when no one is drinking?" It was true. We thought back to our time on the boat docks, and to our many Christmas Eves where the liquor was always flowing. Here and now, no one was drinking. The generation who struggled through their days self-medicated with alcohol had nearly all passed on. The new generation was now in charge. And we were going to be honest and speak the truth. I have nothing but the deepest admiration and respect for Sandy and Marcia. It goes beyond our shared histories. Although we can't stay in as close contact as I would like because of our busy and separate lives, I know I can always talk to them about anything. I think they know that about me too. Every family has problems and we are no different.

My mom had driven up with my brother to our reunion and was one of only two remaining in her generation. The party was at my cousin's home, and Mom was sitting at the kitchen table when I approached her. I was so nervous, I wished I had written down some notes to help me.

"Mom, can you come in the living room with me?"

"What? What do you want? Is something wrong?" she replied.

"No, nothing is wrong. I just want to talk to you."

I guided her into the living room and sat down with her.

"Mom, I don't think . . . I've ever thanked you properly."

"Thanked me? What do you mean?"

"For all you did for me. For everything. For every sacrifice. For changing your life for me. For being tough. For how hard it was. For everything you had to do. For everything and everyone you had to put up with. For protecting me. For guiding me. For every decision you made. I know you did it all because you love me. If you had made any decision differently, who knows what would have happened? You won the Olympic gold medal as much as I did, but I got all the glory. I never could have done it without you. It's taken all these years for me to realize it. Few parents would have given so much to help a child achieve their dream. Most would have said 'no' at some point, admitting that enough is enough. The gold medal was the culmination of your years of hard work and devotion. I want you to have it. You deserve it as much as me."

"Oh, no, honey, you have to have the gold medal." I could tell her eyes were glistening with emotion.

"It's in my attic and I want you to have it."

"No. You keep it."

"I thought you'd say that. That's why I got you this."

I had a jewelry box with me. I gave it to her, and she opened it.

Inside was a golden snowflake pendant studded with diamonds.

"Dorothy, it's beautiful."

She lifted it out of the box and let me put it around her neck, just as officials had put a gold medal around my neck thirty years before.

"This is just a token of my love and appreciation. Please wear it like the medal of honor that you deserve."

She was truly touched. She suddenly didn't look like her anxious, unhappy self. This was a good day for her. And for me. We had our own private medal ceremony.

My brother said she happily talked nonstop about the pendant, and what it meant to her, during their two-hour ride home.

My mother and I have a good relationship now. We are two adults, instead of mother and daughter. I hope I stopped looking for her approval decades ago. I have always treasured her sense of humor. We can laugh together now. She and I share a unique history. And we can look forward to our future. I see our future in my daughter, Alex. She is kind and passionate, extremely sensitive to others, and has inherited a gift for music from my father's side, discovering her singing voice in the sixth grade. She is incredibly capable at only eighteen, managing to surprise me with a well-planned, thoughtful, wonderful fiftieth birthday party this past year, complete with pianist, bartender, a full dinner, and out-of-town guests flown in. But she knows she doesn't need to impress me. She had my unconditional approval the day she was born.

Soon after I gave Mom the golden snowflake, she wrote me a thank-you note:

Dear Dorf [my affectionate nickname in my family, as my brother and sister could not pronounce Dorothy when I was born],

What a lovely surprise present. I truly had tears in my eyes! I love you lots and only wish you had a nice husband. You do have a lovely daughter and you are bringing her up so nicely.

Well, dear, I can't tell you how much you really meant to me and your dad, too. We so wanted you to have everything possible. Who knows where skating will lead. It was a pure miracle.

Love you, Mom

Thank you mom — I love you. We were a miracle. Together.

ACKNOWLEDGMENTS

My deepest thanks to my beautiful daughter, Alex, for being my giant ray of sunshine during my difficult soul searching for this book. I want to express my gratitude to my dear sister, Marcia, for being there for me throughout as my sounding board and my rock, and to my brilliant brother, Sandy, for his knowledge, understanding, and sense of humor. My eternal thanks to Deborah Amelon whose talent, finely honed craft, perseverance, unwavering belief in me, and positive outlook made this book happen. I will always be grateful I could fully put my trust in her. She worked so much harder than I making sense of my life, creating a story from it and finding perspective. Thank you to Rob, Addison, Walker, Jessie, and Maynard for their support, too. Thank you to our editor, Gretchen Young, for encouraging us to delve deeper and helping us blossom with her invaluable contribution. Thank you to Mel Berger for bringing us together. Thank you to Rick Hersh and Ariel Hankin for their integrity, advice, and reassurance. A huge thank you to my girly girlfriends: Andrea Taylor, Georgia Usry, Julia Keelty, and Debbie Gordon — the most incredible women I've ever known — for lifting my spirits when I was at my lowest. Thank you to my best friends, the talented choreographers Tim Murphy and Nathan Birch, for their steadfast love and friendship. Thank you, Dean Moye, for being my voice of reason. Thank you to my dad, whose zest for life still drives me to be the best I can be. Finally, I want to thank my mom for her compassion, her caring, and her incredible memory helping me recall our adventures.